PEARLS GETS PUT IN THE POKEY

Stephan Pastis

A *Pearls Before Swine* Treasury

Andrews McMeel
PUBLISHING®

Pearls Before Swine is distributed internationally by Andrews McMeel Syndication.

Pearls Gets Put in the Pokey copyright © 2024 by Stephan Pastis. All rights reserved. Printed in China. No part of this book may be used or reproduced in any manner whatsoever without written permission except in the case of reprints in the context of reviews.

Andrews McMeel Publishing
a division of Andrews McMeel Universal
1130 Walnut Street, Kansas City, Missouri 64106

www.andrewsmcmeel.com

23 24 25 26 27 SDB 10 9 8 7 6 5 4 3 2 1

ISBN: 978-1-5248-9296-8

Library of Congress Control Number: 2024933611

Pearls Before Swine can be viewed on the internet at www.pearlscomic.com.

These strips appeared in newspapers from October 11, 2021 to April 9, 2023.

Editor: Betty Wong
Creative Director: Julie Phillips
Photographer: Ryan Schude
Cover Design: Donna Oatney
Text Design: Brittany Lee

Production Editor: Jasmine Lim
Production Manager: Chadd Keim

PEARLS GETS PUT IN THE POKEY

Other *Pearls Before Swine* Collections

Treasuries

Gift Books

Kids' Books

Dedication

To Charles Schulz
For a lifetime of inspiration

Introduction

I was in third grade when I first found these *Peanuts* books on my Aunt Angela's shelf:

All of which I borrowed, none of which I returned. And some of which, as in *Here Comes Snoopy*, I read until the cover slipped off. Because there was something about Charlie Brown's adult-free world that I loved—the humor, the darkness, the characters, the maturity.

And I wasn't done.

Because I then headed to my public library for more, which I know for a fact because their summer reading program made students keep track of the books they'd read on a little card. And my list had a *Peanuts* book (*Speak Softly, and Carry a Beagle*) sitting prominently at no. 5:

The idea of the reading program was to give the students of San Marino, California, an early love of literature, which they incentivized by awarding certificates to students who'd read ten books by the end of the summer.

But young me had discovered a loophole:

Peanuts comic strips counted.

And so, two more *Peanuts* comic strip collections (*You're Something Else, Charlie Brown,* and *You're Out of Your Mind, Charlie Brown!*) occupied slot nos. 7 and 10 on my rapidly expanding list of great literature:

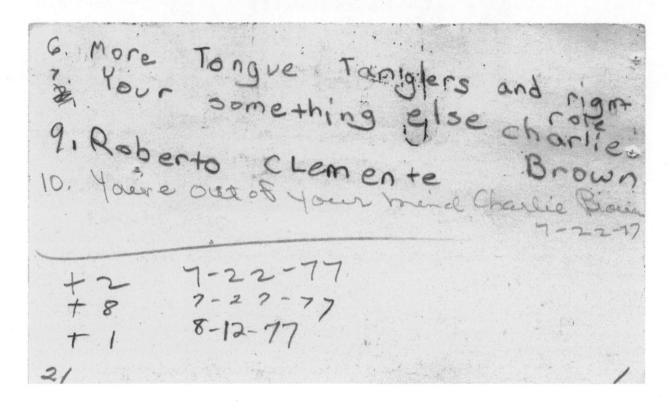

And it was a list, as you can see from the above, that did not even have a no. 8, as I had apparently found yet another loophole:

I could count blank space as a book.

After the first ten books, the list gave me credit for eleven more. And although the titles of them weren't specified on the card, I have no doubt they were mostly more *Peanuts* books.

And perhaps another blank space.

For I had gamed the system.

And by the end of summer had gotten my certificate (below), which read, "Stephan Pastis has completed the Summer Vacation Reading requirements," but more accurately should have read, "Just learned a whole lot about comic strips."

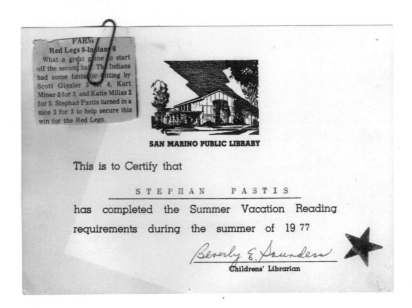

SAN MARINO PUBLIC LIBRARY

This is to Certify that

S T E P H A N   P A S T I S

has completed the Summer Vacation Reading requirements during the summer of 19 77

Beverly E. Saunders
Childrens' Librarian

FARM
Red Legs 8-Indians 6
What a great game to start off the second half. The Indians had some fantastic hitting by Scott Giesler 3 for 4, Kurt Miner 2 for 3, and Katie Milias 2 for 3. Stephan Pastis turned in a nice 2 for 3 to help secure this win for the Red Legs.

My favorite part about the certificate is that my mother not only saved it but made sure to attach a newspaper clipping to it from one of my Little League games noting I had "turned in a nice 2 for 3 to help secure [a] win for the Red Legs."

And I was one charming Red Leg:

(Young Stephan laughing at his defrauding of the San Marino Public Library's summer reading program.)

But as prolific as my baseball career was, my first love was cartooning.

Because from the moment I first read *Peanuts*, all I wanted to do was draw. Which I did.

And soon after got one of my drawings published in my elementary school paper, the *Carver Carverette* (below, lower right):

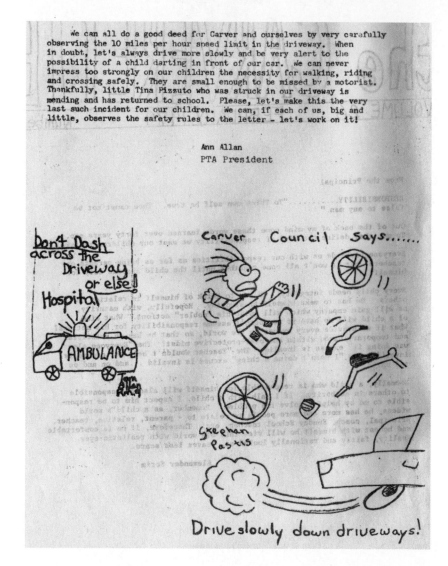

It was perhaps fitting, given my career that would one day follow, that the drawing was (A) dark (a person hit by a car); and (B) made fun of cyclists (there'd be a lifetime of that ahead).

And grim as it was, it was nowhere near as dark as the stuff I drew at home. For while other nine-year-olds drew puppies and rainbows, I drew John F. Kennedy shortly before his assassination in Dallas:

. . . Which should have sent me straight to therapy.

But instead, my mother opted to save the cash and just let me keep drawing.

Which I did—through middle school, high school, college, and law school at UCLA, where during a class on the European Economic Community, I first drew a character called Rat, shown below in a strip that was clearly not ready for newspapers:

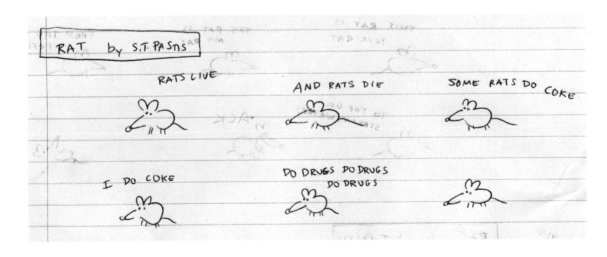

In fact, the Rat strips I drew in my law school classes were so bad and nonsensical that one of the students sitting next to me scrawled "stupid" across the page:

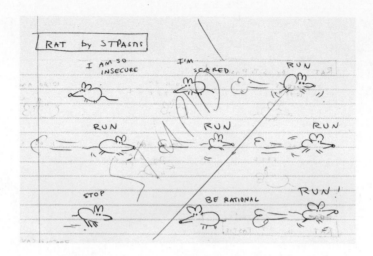

Which was fair. Since it was bad. And odd.

And thus, I had little hope of ever being a syndicated cartoonist like my idol, Charles Schulz.

For even if a person is good at drawing and capable of writing jokes, comic strip syndicates get thousands of submissions every year, out of which they might pick one for newspapers. And even if a strip does make it into newspapers, something like five out of every six comics fail within their first few years.

So the odds were very much against me.

And so, I went on to a career I didn't much like, that of a lawyer, which for me was a bit of a prison creatively—as it seemed both unimaginative and uninspiring. So to survive, I continued drawing in my free time, at night after work and on weekends, hoping that one day I could turn my childhood dream of cartooning into a reality and escape the law.

All of which brings me back to my Little League career, and my Red Legs coach, Mr. Drellashik, who at the end of the season asked me if I was going anywhere for summer vacation. And I told him that yes, we were visiting some relatives "back east," a term I had learned from my California parents for anywhere east of Bakersfield.

And he said, "Where back east?"

"Ohio," I answered.

"That's where my relatives are," he said. "Do you know which part?"

"Cleveland."

"That's where mine are. Do you know where in Cleveland?"

"Some part called Rocky River."

"That's where *mine* are!" repeated Coach Drellashik, both of us rather amazed at the coincidence.

And so summer came, and we traveled to our relatives' house in Rocky River, and I played football with my cousin in his backyard. It was a yard that was much different than the ones I was used to in California in that there were no fences. So when my cousin overthrew the football, I asked if I could run into his neighbor's yard to get it.

"Sure," he said, "Mr. Drellashik wouldn't mind."

That's right.

My relatives lived *next door* to my coach's.

The odds of which were about 100,000,000 to 1.

But what are odds if not something to be defied?

And so, after many years of being a lawyer, I finally got up the courage to submit a strip I'd drawn about a rat and a pig called *Pearls Before Swine* to United Feature Syndicate, the same company that syndicated *Peanuts*—the strip that for me had started it all.

And they accepted it.

And I was free.

Stephan Pastis
October 2024

Make every day better than the last!

NOT HARD WHEN THE DAYS ARE AS CRAPPY AS THESE.

PLEASE DON'T WRITE IN MY MOTIVATIONAL DIARY.

Because you bought this treasury, your days will now be much less crappy. Or perhaps crappier. Always hard to say.

WHAT ARE YOU WATCHING, RAT?

OUR NATIONAL PASTIME.

I JUST LOVE THE CRACK OF THE BAT, THE HITTING, THE RUNNING, THE STEALING.

BASEBALL DOES HOLD US ALL TOGETHER.

BASEBALL? I'M WATCHING RIOTING.

THINGS HAVE CHANGED IN THIS COUNTRY.

OH, YEAH. BASEBALL WAS MUCH LESS EXCITING.

Speaking of baseball, I have every single Topps baseball card from 1975 to 1985. And that's the kind of gripping insight you will find in this treasury.

OH, MY GOODNESS! I'M SO HAPPY ABOUT THIS DATE I'M ABOUT TO GO ON I DON'T KNOW WHAT TO DO!

YOU CAN'T MEET HER IN THAT STATE. YOU'LL MAKE A FOOL OF YOURSELF.

THEN WHAT DO I DO? WHAT DO I DO? I'M JUST SO HAPPY!

HANG ON. I KEEP A 'NEW YORK TIMES' REPORTER HERE FOR JUST THIS OCCASION.

EVERYONE'S DYING AND THE WORLD IS ENDING.

HEY. IT WORKED.

YEAH, THEY CAN REALLY BRING YOU DOWN.

I always hesitate to put actual years in *Pearls*, as I think it tends to date the strips when they appear later in books. So go ahead and cross out the years I wrote and put in more recent ones.

I really should tweet that and see what happens.

If you're wondering how to draw Rat's sisters, do the following:
(1) Draw Rat;
(2) Add hair.

Panel 1: I WAS WITH A FRIEND OF MINE THIS MORNING. I THINK I SOLVED ALL OF HER PROBLEMS. / OH YEAH? HOW?

Panel 2: I STOPPED CAUSING THEM.

Panel 3: I DON'T THINK YOU GET CREDIT FOR THAT. / SHE SEEMED GRATEFUL.

Panel 1: DID YOU HEAR THIS STORY ABOUT THE BAD STUFF THIS ACTRESS DID? / HOW DO YOU KNOW IT'S TRUE?

Panel 2: I SAW IT ON THE TWITTER. / BUT TWITTER DOESN'T VERIFY THAT IT'S TRUE.

Panel 3: YES IT DOES. THEY EMPLOY THOUSANDS OF PEOPLE WHO VERIFY THE TRUTH OF EACH STORY BEFORE IT GETS TWEETED OUT. / WHERE DID YOU HEAR THAT?

Panel 4: ON THE TWITTER. / NO. / SOUNDS RIGHT. I'LL TWEET THAT.

There are a lot of strips making fun of Twitter in this book. So, if your name is Elon Musk, consider this a trigger warning.

Panel 1: HI, ALLY ACTRESS. WHAT ARE YOU UP TO TODAY? / GOTTA GO TAKE SOME HEADSHOTS.

Panel 2: OH, WELL, GOOD TO TALK TO YOU, BUT I GOTTA GET GOING.

Panel 4: I JUST AVERTED TRAGEDY.

Grim transition, but speaking of headshots, I recently visited the site of John F. Kennedy's assassination in Dallas, Texas. On the next page is the window from which Lee Harvey Oswald fired the fatal shots. Or didn't. Depending on which conspiracy theory you believe. All I know for sure is that I was not involved.

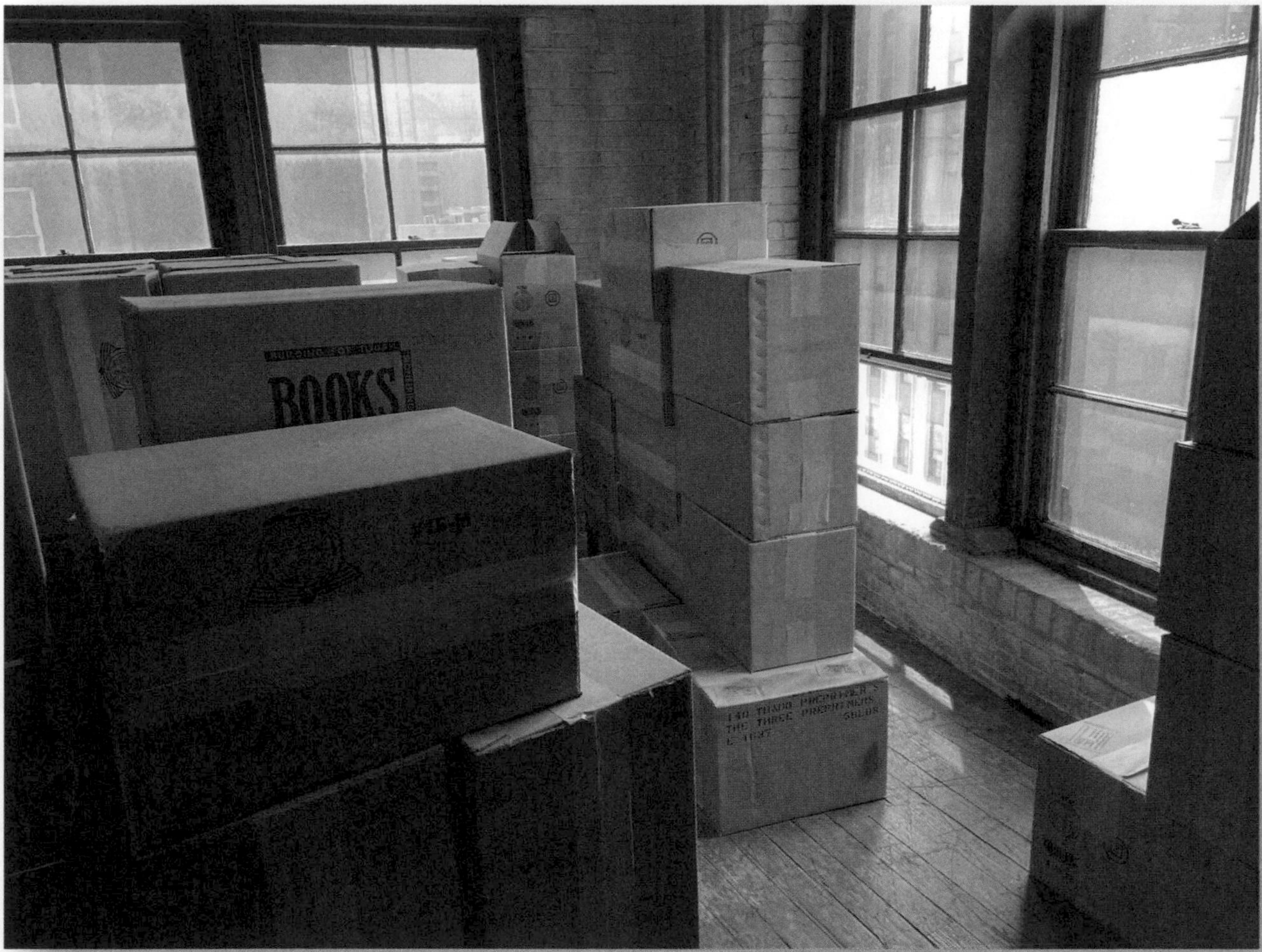
BOOKS

I'm so old that I had to check with my nieces Elenique and Kali to make sure #livingmybestlife was a popular hashtag. Also, it bears mentioning that I am their favorite uncle, which I can say without fear of contradiction because they're not allowed to type words in this book.

I recently found myself in the Ozark Mountains when suddenly my iPhone lost all service, meaning I could no longer navigate. But, like most people, I never carry maps on trips anymore. So I had to just remember that the sun sets in the east and head that direction.

Note regarding that last comment: My editor, Betty Wong, informs me that the sun sets mostly in the west.

I think I screwed this one up because in the sixth and seventh panels, it's not really clear that Pig walked *through* the portal. He might have just walked past it. Oh, well. I can't be a brilliant genius all the time.

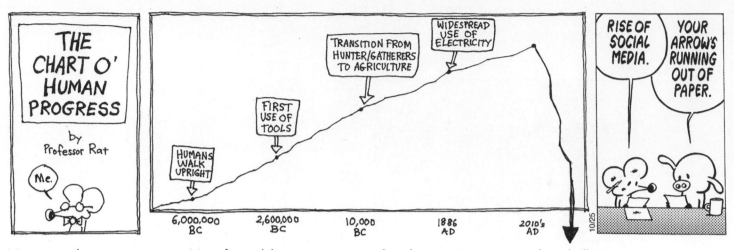

Note regarding prior comment: My wife read the commentary and said, "I've never seen you be a brilliant genius even once."

This really seemed to happen toward the end of every Halloween night. And like Rat, I gave them all our remaining candy.

Aww. I really do wish someone had told me that.

I don't believe you're allowed to say "homeless" anymore, so I'm guessing "hobo" is out too. I will go ahead and cancel myself now.

Once, at my uncle's funeral, one of the priests asked for my autograph as I was about to carry the coffin. It was odd.

Because of my Jef the Cyclist strips, I am constantly asked by cyclists to please portray them in a more favorable light. I have yet to do so.

24

I recently went on a three-week trip, and when I got back, I discovered that a block of mozzarella cheese I had kept in the refrigerator had gone bad. I had no choice but to throw it out. To this day, it's the most tragic thing that's ever happened to me.

While I have never personally stolen a corpse, the great artist Leonardo DaVinci apparently *did*. Or at least paid others to do it for him. He wanted the cadavers so he could study human anatomy.

I wrote this strip after a number of friends told me about stuff like this happening to them. They would talk about a trip with a friend, and ads for such a trip would start showing up on their social media feeds.

Row 1 panels:

Self-Improvement Worksheet

All of us should strive to be a professional in everything we do.

Because being a pro means being:
PROactive
PROductive
PROmising
PROud

In what ways are you a pro?

I PROcrastinate.

GOOD TO KNOW I'M A PRO AT SOMETHING.

Row 2 panels:

PLAN FOR LIFE
-Publish novel by age 30.
-Win Pulitzer by 35.
-Become millionaire by 40.
-Retire by 45.
-Travel entire world by 50.

WHAT'S ALL THAT, NEIGHBOR NED?

MY PLAN FOR LIFE. YOU SHOULD DO ONE, TOO.

Eat pizza by 6 (o'clock)

HARD FOR ME TO SEE PAST DINNER.

In 2021, I took a wild chance and submitted my comic strip for a Pulitzer Prize. I did not win. But even better, *nobody* won, as the judges determined that no cartoonist was worthy of a prize that year. I like to think that they took one look at my entry and left in disgust.

Row 3 panels:

WELL, MY TRAVEL PLANS ARE SET. GONNA HEAD TO SPAIN AND PORTUGAL. HOW ABOUT YOU? ARE YOU GOING ANYWHERE?

OH...WELL... I'M THINKING OF GOING SOMEWHERE GREAT.

LIKE MAYBE.... MONEY ISLAND, WHERE I CAN FIND STACKS OF CASH TO SEE EUROPE !!!

MAYBE I'LL DISCUSS THIS WITH SOMEONE ELSE.

NO, GO ON, MR. PRIVILEGED.

I recently went to Madrid with my niece. We both got drunk and passed out in a park. I should mention that she's almost forty, and not five years old.

11/7

In theory, he could have just let go of the balloon. But then I wouldn't have this comic strip.
So please, suspend your disbelief.

WHAT ARE YOU DOING, RAT?

SELLING MY MICROWAVE, MY STOVE, AND MY CAR.

OH YEAH, WHY? ARE YOU GETTING NEW ONES?

NOPE.

I AM ELIMINATING ALL THREE DEVICES FROM MY LIFE FOREVER.

SOME GUYS HATE CHANGING THE CLOCKS MORE THAN OTHERS.

DON'T THINK I DON'T SEE YOU, COFFEE MAKER!

Hulloooo, Larry wife. Me kill a cheeken for you dinner.

WELL, THANK YOU, BOB. HOW VERY KIND.

You beleev dat? He buy from ressraunt.

YES, LARRY, I BELIEVE IT. HE'S A SKILLED HUNTER.

Me kill a cole slaw.

HOW YOU DOING, PIG?

GREAT. I FINALLY RENTED THIS APARTMENT I OWN TO TWO GUYS WHO DRESS LIKE EVEL KNIEVEL.

SO YOU'RE THE LESSOR OF TWO EVELS.

MAY ALL YOUR STUNTS GO AWRY.

Because I'm a bit obsessed with death, I recently sought out and found the grave of the former daredevil, Evel Knievel. It's located in Butte, Montana. And because I know you will probably not seek it out yourself, I present it to you on the next page:

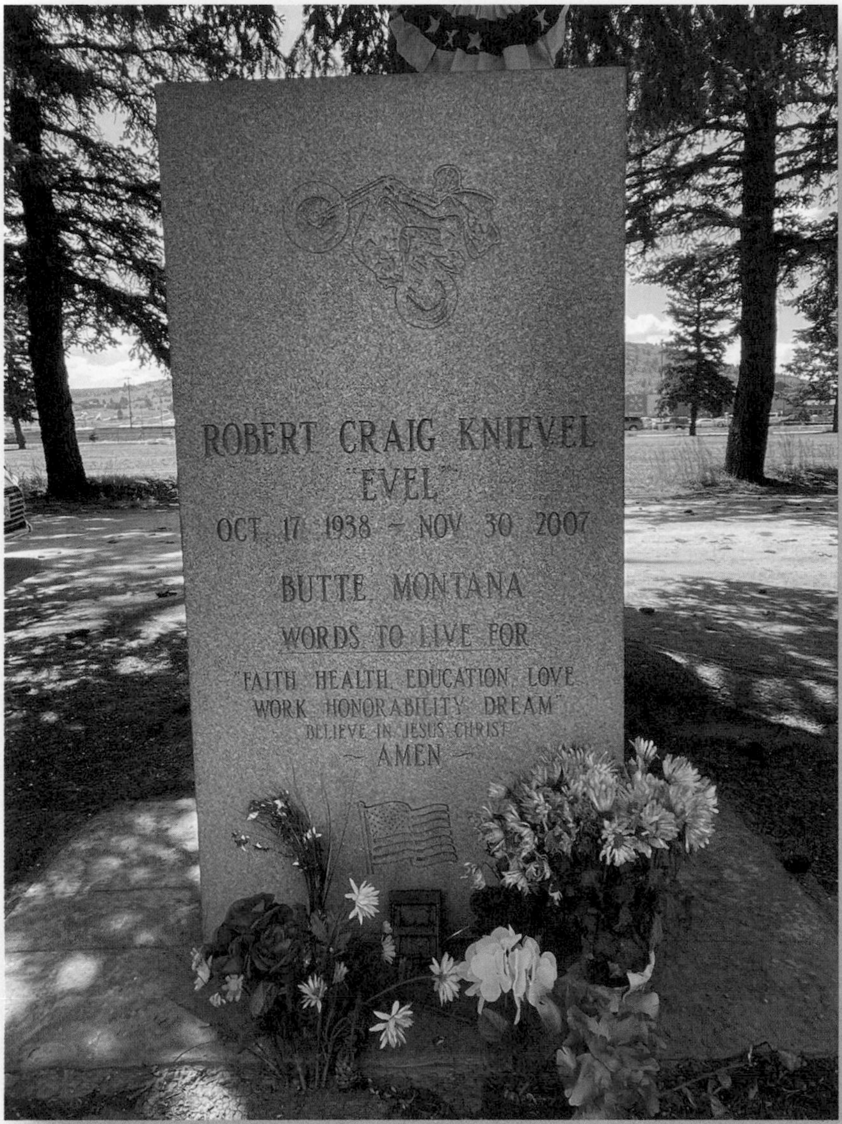
ROBERT CRAIG KNIEVEL
"EVEL"
OCT 17 1938 – NOV 30 2007
BUTTE MONTANA
WORDS TO LIVE FOR
"FAITH HEALTH EDUCATION LOVE
WORK HONORABILITY DREAM"
BELIEVE IN JESUS CHRIST
~ AMEN ~

WHAT ARE THE ISSUES IN THIS COUNTRY THAT WORRY YOU THE MOST?

THERE'S THIS BIG CHUNK OF LAND AT THE TOP OF WISCONSIN THAT DOESN'T EVEN TOUCH MICHIGAN, AND YET SOMEHOW MICHIGAN TOOK IT.

I FEAR WISCONSIN FIGHTING THEM FOR IT.

WASN'T ONE OF MY TOP TEN ISSUES.

DO YOU SUPPOSE THEY'LL HIT THEM WITH CHEESE WHEELS?

Seriously, look at a map. It's very odd.

WHAT KEEPS ME FROM BEING AS SUCCESSFUL AS I COULD BE?

FEAR OF FAILING. ELIMINATE IT.

FEAR?

FAILING.

ADVICE IS OVERRATED.

HEY, RAT, WHAT'S WITH THE HALO? YOU SUDDENLY TRYING TO CONVINCE US THAT YOU'RE GOOD?

WHAT ARE YOU TALKING ABOUT?

SORRY.

IT'S SO HARD TO GAUGE TIME IN COMIC STRIPS.

This particular strip is very strange. Just move on to the next one and erase it from your consciousness.

30

11/14

I like to think that Tim Cook saw this strip and has it framed in his office. I also like to think he goes around kicking people in the testicles.

Lately, I've determined that I like dogs much more than people. Except you. You seem nice.

I once had a reader ask what it is that gets all over Pig's face when he writes. I thought it was fairly obvious that it was ink. So put that person in the category of people I don't like.

There's a great book on professional Scrabble players called *Word Freak*. Also great is the fact that the author's name sounds just like mine—Stefan Fatsis.

This seems to happen to me all the time. A character on a show gets a text or a call and I check my phone. Then I feel very stupid. Even more so than usual.

Since my strip is fairly deadpan, the characters typically show no expression, which would generally be indicated by eyebrows (I rarely use them) and mouths (I rarely show them). So it's fun sometimes to draw Pig with huge eyes and a wide open mouth.

THIS STUDY SAYS OPTIMISTS LIVE LONGER.

AND YET THEY STILL DIE.

PESSIMISM IS ALWAYS THE ANSWER.

I'm an optimist who knows I will always be disappointed.

WARNING: BEARS IN AREA

WARNING: RATTLESNAKES

WARNING: UNINFORMED PEOPLE MAY START SPOUTING THEIR OPINIONS

WANT TO HEAR WHAT I THINK OF THE GOVERNMENT?

THAT WAS TERRIFYING.

I was recently in Bangkok, Thailand, when I found a relaxing park with a lake. So I sat on the grass by the shore. Then I saw a sign warning about giant monitor lizards in the lake. This ended my relaxing time in the park.

DO YOU EVER THINK THAT YOUR LIFE THIS PAST YEAR HAS JUST BEEN TOO DARN BORING?

I GUESS IT DEPENDS ON HOW YOU DEFINE THE WORD.

LOOK IT UP IN THE DICTIONARY.

boring (*adj.*)
your life

THAT HURTS.

35

HEY, NEIGHBOR NANCY, HOW'S IT GOING?

VERY WELL, THANK YOU...MY FIANCÉ JUST GOT ACCEPTED INTO BROWN UNIVERSITY.

THAT'S WONDERFUL. IS HE TRAINING TO BE A U.P.S. DRIVER?

NOT WHERE THEY'RE TRAINED.

IS HE HANDSOME WITH MEATY THIGHS?

FRIED CHICKEN AND BEER, HUH? A DIET LIKE THAT WILL TAKE TEN YEARS OFF YOUR LIFE, YOU FOOL.

IF THE PURPOSE OF YOUR LIFE IS JUST TO PROLONG YOUR LIFE, THEN MAYBE THERE'S NOT MUCH LIFE TO PROLONG.

GOOD THING YOU HAVE TEN EXTRA YEARS TO THINK OF A COMEBACK.

YOU WAIT. IT'S COMING.

My one big dietary weakness in life is bread. I will buy a whole loaf and just walk around taking bites out of it.

HEY, GOAT, HAVE YOU MET OUR NEW PET, 'PSYCHO KILLER BUNNY'?

HAHA. NO, BUT I LOVE THE NAME.

DIE! **DIE!** **DIE!**

HOP HOP HOP

NEVER CONDESCEND TO 'PSYCHO KILLER BUNNY.'

The bunny in the second panel was just a sketch I drew one day. I liked it, so I turned it into a strip. Maybe I should make him a regular character.

I worry sometimes about people who are new readers seeing a strip like this and wondering what the hell is going on in the last panel. I.e., who is the rat hitting? And why? Thus, I put my last name on the little placard there so that they know he's hitting the creator of the strip.

I really should make inspirational posters.

I did this strip after visiting Philadelphia and learning that the cheese they often use on their famous cheesesteaks is none other than Cheez Whiz. Which, by the way, tasted great.

Speaking of free food, I often engage my son Thomas in debates over how many free mints you can take from a restaurant before they would stop you. He thinks it's anything more than a fistful. My theory is that you're fine until you start pouring them into a bucket. One day I plan on testing these theories. He has asked to be nowhere near me when I do.

From the Department of How the Hell Did This Happen: If this strip seems familiar, it's because I ran almost the identical strip two weeks earlier on November 19. The only thing I can't figure out is that (1) I had the joke written out on notebook paper and mistakenly drew it a second time; or (2) I really have lost it. My money's on the latter.

Little did you know that pencils make a "write write write" sound when you use them.

WELL, NEIGHBOR BOB, YOU SURE LOOK HAPPY FOR A GUY I JUST EVISCERATED ON TWITTER. DON'T ACT LIKE IT DIDN'T AFFECT YOU.

I GAVE UP SOCIAL MEDIA YEARS AGO. I'VE BEEN HAPPY EVER SINCE.

THAT DOESN'T SEEM FAIR.

As I'm writing this in July of 2023, it's not clear what will happen to Twitter. But if it does go away, I don't think I'll miss it.

HEY, RAT, SINCE WHEN DO YOU WATCH THAT NEWS CHANNEL? / I LIKE TO CHECK IN ON IT NOW AND THEN.

TO BE EXPOSED TO A WIDER VARIETY OF OPINION AND HELP YOU KEEP AN OPEN MIND?

TO CONFIRM THEY'RE STILL NUTTERS.

THAT'S ALMOST OPEN-MINDED. / OH, LOOK, THEY'RE STILL NUTTERS.

"Nutters" is a great, underutilized word. The Brits use it all the time.

Dear Powers That Be in the Universe...

How is it that you can just have me die unexpectedly at any given moment?

And yet the power company has to warn me when just shutting off the power?

SOMETIMES I CAN BE SO PROFOUND.

This one makes me laugh. I can say that now and then and there's really nothing you can do to stop me.

This one makes me laugh.

This one makes me laugh.

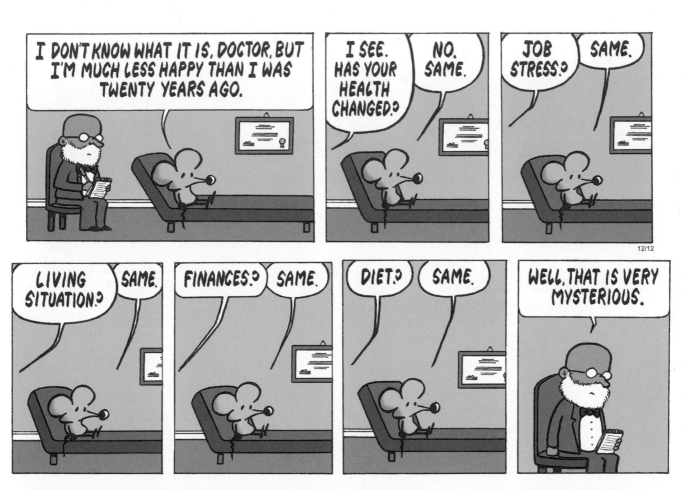

I've never been to a therapist. But around a hundred people who know me have told me that I should go. Surely, they're all wrong.

I did a lot of strips about the pandemic in 2020 and 2021. It was simply too big a part of our lives to ignore.

It's hard to do strips about snowmen and not think about *Calvin and Hobbes*. I think Bill Watterson more or less owns the snowman genre.

Dear Reader: Due to supply chain issues, there will be no jokes in today's comic, as all of our jokes are currently stuck in shipping containers overseas. Please feel free to fill in your own. Thanks for your patience.

I was surprised at how many people actually filled in the blank speech balloons and sent them to me. Maybe I should do it every day and save myself a lot of time.

Speaking of death, I visit a whole lot of graves. In just the past few years, I've gone to the graves of Abraham Lincoln, Mark Twain, Buddy Holly, Lyndon Johnson, Woodrow Wilson, George H.W. Bush, Grover Cleveland, Dwight Eisenhower, Herbert Hoover, Susan B. Anthony, Franklin and Eleanor Roosevelt, Lee Harvey Oswald, Aaron Burr, Ben Franklin, *Twilight Zone* creator Rod Serling, Fred Rogers (aka Mr. Rogers), Kit Carson, Joseph Smith (founder of Mormonism), Charles Schulz, Wild Bill Hickok, Uncle Sam (he was a real man), Lucille Ball, Frederick Douglass, Elvis Presley, author John Kennedy Toole, and Nicolas Cage, who, while not dead, has already had his grave built in New Orleans.

Below is Lincoln's grave in Springfield, Illinois. Consider it a rough model for how I'd like my own to one day look.

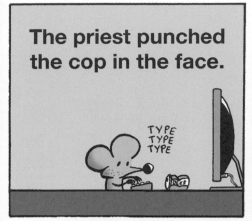

And believe it or not, Rat's writing is way more comprehensible than *Ulysses* by James Joyce. I defy you to read it and make sense of it.

INSPIRATION
FOR
TODAY:

None.

SOME DAYS RETURNING TO
BED IS THE BEST OPTION.

I DON'T UNDERSTAND HALF THIS
COUNTRY OR HOW THEY THINK.

HOW MUCH
WAS THAT
SLICE OF
TOAST?

SIX
DOLLARS.
IT'S
ARTISANAL.

MAYBE THE
ISSUE'S
NOT
THEM.

IS THAT
FRENCH
FOR
'RIP-OFF'?

I drew this strip after visiting the heartland of America—namely, the Great Plains states of Nebraska, Kansas, North Dakota, and South Dakota. It was much different than where I live in California and gave me a new perspective.

HEY, NEIGHBOR BOB, WHO'S YOUR
FRIEND THERE?

OH, I MET HIM AT AN AQUARIUM.
WE GO EVERYWHERE TOGETHER.

MUST BE NICE TO HAVE A PORPOISE
IN LIFE.

Panel 1: AND WHAT CAN I GET YOU THIS CHRISTMAS? / A CHOO-CHOO TRAIN!

Panel 2: A WONDERFUL GIFT! MERRY CHRISTMAS TO YOU!

Panel 3: AND WHAT CAN I GET YOU THIS CHRISTMAS? / NO MORE CRAP YEARS LOST TO COVID.

Panel 4: DO WE MAKE THOSE? / I'LL GIVE HIM BOOZE.

I don't do many Christmas strips. The reason is that I'm generally around seven months ahead of deadline, and it's hard to think Christmassy thoughts in May.

Panel 1: WELL, I'M OFF TO GET SOME BROTH AT A PLACE RAT TOLD ME ABOUT. / HAVE FUN.

Panel 3: TURNS OUT THAT'S NOT WHAT BROTHELS SELL.

Panel 1: HEY, RAT, PIG IS GONNA HELP ME MOVE TO MY NEW PLACE ON SUNDAY. MIND HELPING AS WELL?

Panel 2: SORRY. CAN'T. / WHY NOT?

Panel 3: BECAUSE THE KIND OF FRIENDS YOU ASK TO HELP YOU MOVE ARE YOUR VERY CLOSEST. AND I'M JUST NOT READY FOR THAT LEVEL OF COMMITMENT.

Panel 4: HARD NOT TO APPRECIATE THE CANDOR. / ALSO, I'M LAZY AND MOVING SUCKS.

It's nice to be able to say "sucks" now and then because it was a word that wasn't allowed on the comics page when I first started out.

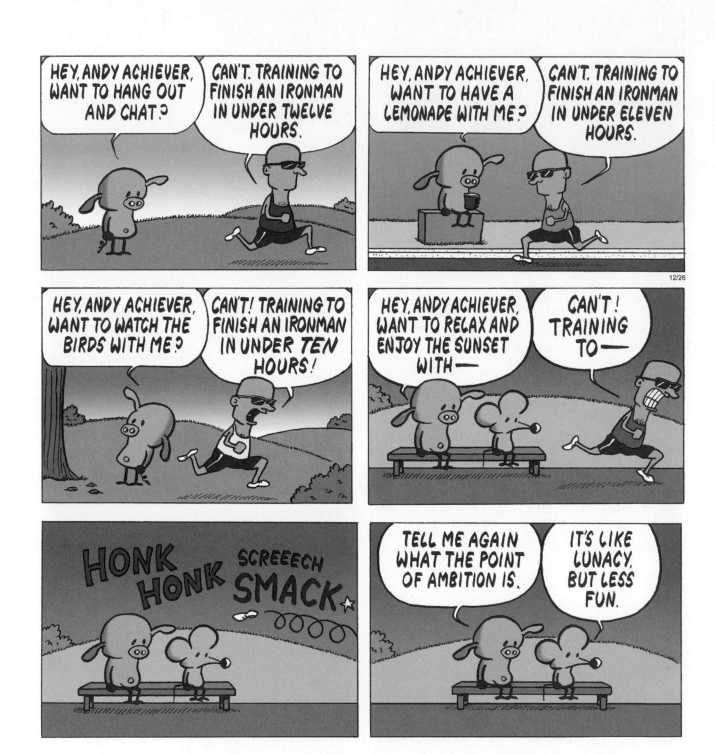

While Andy Achiever appears to change his shirt from panel to panel, he apparently never changes his shorts. Good thing he's gone.

MONDAY
MOTIVATION

DREAMS *DO*
COME TRUE!

Mostly
for other
people.

Fortunately,
the rest
of us have
cheese.

I'm still sad about that block of mozzarella cheese that I lost. If you see me at a book signing, please bring me a block of mozzarella cheese.

HEY GONESOON, DO YOU EVER WONDER WHAT YOUR LEGACY WILL BE AFTER YOU'RE GONE?

A PUDDLE AND A CARROT.

SOME GUYS HAVE MODEST AMBITIONS.

I would like my legacy to be a grave that is even larger than Lincoln's, though I suspect my wife Staci will instead save the cash and use it on a new kitchen. If you see my grave and it's small, you know what happened.

DO YOU EVER TRY TO IMPROVE THE KIND OF GUY YOU ARE?

SURE. RIGHT NOW I'M WORKING ON OVERCOMING JEALOUSY.

GOOD FOR YOU. HOW ARE YOU DOING IT?

BY BECOMING SO SUPERIOR TO OTHERS THAT I HAVE NOTHING TO BE JEALOUS OF.

I DON'T KNOW IF THAT COUNTS.

YOU'RE JEALOUS I THOUGHT OF IT FIRST.

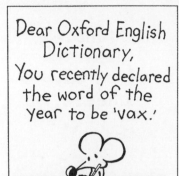

Dear Oxford English Dictionary, You recently declared the word of the year to be 'vax.'

This was in error.

The word of the year is 'crappo.' As in, 'This year was crappo.'

IT WAS LAST YEAR'S ALSO.

WELL, NO MORE BEING POOR FOR ME... I'M OFF TO BUY FIFTY BUCKS' WORTH OF LOTTERY TICKETS AT THE GROCERY STORE.

PIG, THE ODDS OF YOU WINNING ARE TERRIBLE. YOU'RE 20,000 TIMES MORE LIKELY TO GET HIT BY LIGHTNING.

OH. THEN I WON'T GO.

'CAUSE YOU DON'T WANT TO WASTE YOUR MONEY?

I DON'T WANT TO GET HIT BY LIGHTNING.

LET'S START OVER.

NOW I'M POOR AND TERRIFIED.

While on my travels, I learned of one of the greatest monuments ever. It is called the Tent Pole Monument to Circus Dead. Located in Wahpeton, North Dakota, it is a tribute to circus workers who were killed by lightning. The monument is a circus tent pole shattered by lightning.

NEW YEAR'S RESOLUTIONS
Reach all of my fitness goals.

Fitness Goals:

Get not that much fatter.

I LIKE TO KEEP THEM WITHIN REACH.

Regarding that last comment: I would like my legacy to be a grave at least as big as the Tent Pole Monument to Circus Dead.

I think I've used Mountain Dew in no fewer than four or five pun strips. But it's a useful pun word, so what else can I dew?

Boney Bone is arguably the most subtextually inappropriate character I've ever created.

And so, just like that, Boney Bone had to go.

Looking back, it's rather amazing how angry people got at both those who wore masks and those who did not. We were (and still are) a very divided country.

I had a friend once lose his keys and turn my cousin's house upside down in search of them. So my cousin sat down with him and said, "Okay, where did you see them last?" And my friend pointed and said, "Right next to that couch." And my cousin replied, "Right by those keys that are sitting next to the couch?"

This was a popular strip, mostly because of the fact that by January 2022, the country had opened up and closed down a number of times, and I think people were just tired of it.

HEY, RAT, IT'S ME, GOAT. WONDERING IF YOU'RE GONNA JOIN US FOR OUR LITTLE GET-TOGETHER.

LOVE TO, BUT I'M AFRAID OF CATCHING COVID.

IT'S VIA ZOOM.

YOU NEVER KNOW.

I'M RUNNING OUT OF EXCUSES.

I'M NOT HAPPY WITH MY LIFE!

WHAT ARE YOU DOING?

MEGAPHONES ARE THE NEXT BEST THING TO THERAPY.

CHOOSE THERAPY INSTEAD.

TRIED. TOO EXPENSIVE.

When I draw the comic, I use a Kuretake brush pen. But when the characters yell, I use a Sharpie. That may not be that interesting, but sometimes I just run out of things to say.

HEY, PIG, I'M SORT OF AFRAID TO ASK BECAUSE YOU HAVEN'T TALKED ABOUT HER IN A WHILE, BUT IS EVERYTHING OKAY WITH YOUR GRANDMA?

OH, THANK YOU, GOAT, BUT YEAH, SHE'S IN A BETTER PLACE NOW.

OH MY GOODNESS, I'M SORRY, PIG. I'M SO, SO SORRY.

ODD REACTION TO GRANDMA BUYING A CONDO.

Originally that last comment read, "Sometimes I run out of shit to say." But my editor, Betty Wong, said that you can't say "shit" in a treasury book. So rest assured, you will not be seeing the word "shit" here.

Sometimes I purposely pronounce the "L" in "could." It sounds like "cooled" and confuses everyone around me.

The way you know that is a raisin is that he comes out of a box marked "raisins." Otherwise, you might think he was a potato.

I am addicted to walking three miles a day. And on trips, I often walk up to nine or ten.
Perhaps I should spend less time walking and more time learning how to draw raisins.

PIG, IT'S MONDAY MORNING. AREN'T YOU GONNA GET OUT OF BED AND GO TO WORK? / NO CHANCE.

WHY NOT? / BECAUSE IN LIFE, THERE'S A 1 IN 112,000 CHANCE OF BEING KILLED BY A VENDING MACHINE.

HIS EXCUSES ARE GETTING FLIMSIER.

And yet, it almost happened to me! I was in a hotel in northern Canada and the candy bar I bought from a vending machine got hung up on something. So me and a friend started rocking it, and dammit, that thing came close to crushing me like a grape. The good news is that I got the candy bar.

Advice O' The Day:
Always be yourself.

Unless yourself is a jerkface.

Then always be someone else.

SOME ADVICE NEEDS TO BE TAILORED.

OH, PIG... IT'S WHAT'S ON THE INSIDE THAT COUNTS.

HELP ME... I NEVER LOOK AS GOOD AS EVERYONE ELSE

... FOR THINGS I'VE LOST, WHICH IS WHY I CAN'T FIND MY CAR KEYS.

SOMEHOW YOU DIDN'T HELP.

Disclaimer from Andrew McMeel Publishing's legal department regarding that last comment: Tipping or rocking a vending machine can result in serious injury or even death. Do not take life advice from Stephan Pastis.

This strip was inspired by a chalkboard I found in a neighborhood in Portland, Oregon. It said, "Before I die I want to _____" and invited people to fill in the blank. I liked it so much that we used it in the film I cowrote called *Timmy Failure: Mistakes Were Made.*

From the Department of Maybe I'm Not Normal: When I write the comic strip in my studio, I have to make sure the tissues are not sticking up from the tissue box, as tissues normally are. If I see them like that, I tuck them into the box.

OH, WISE ASS ON THE HILL, PEOPLE ON THE RIGHT HATE THE LEFT. PEOPLE ON THE LEFT HATE THE RIGHT. AND THE MEDIA MAKES EVERYONE HATE EVERYONE MORE.

IN 1990, THERE WERE 60 BILLIONAIRES IN THE U.S.... TODAY THERE ARE 664. TOGETHER THOSE 664 PEOPLE HAVE MORE MONEY THAN THE BOTTOM 165,000,000 AMERICANS COMBINED.

AND THE THING THOSE 664 PEOPLE FEAR THE MOST IS THAT ONE DAY THOSE 165,000,000 PEOPLE ON THE RIGHT AND LEFT ARE GONNA SEE THEY HAVE MORE IN COMMON THAN THEY REALIZE.... SO THE RICH DIVIDE THEM.

WHY DOESN'T EVERYONE KNOW THAT?

BECAUSE THE RICH OWN THE MEDIA. AND IF YOU SAY ANYTHING, THEY'LL CRUSH YOU AND REPLACE Y

AND WE RIPPED UP THE BAD MAN'S COMIC WHY?

'CAUSE HE'S A COMMUNISS?

AND HE'S GOING STRAIGHT TO HELL, JEFFY.

This was the most popular comic of the year. And those stats really are true.

Hallmark: Please license this as a New Year's card.

True Fact: I can't be friends with anyone who needs more than four words to order a coffee.

I think I've mentioned this in a prior treasury book, but when the world shut down in early 2020, I was in Medellín, Colombia, where I almost got stuck. Also, I am not a cocaine dealer.

It appears I had this phase where I wasn't using any backgrounds, as you can see in panels (1) through (3). I'm not sure why I did that, and it looks sort of odd to me now. Also, I really am not a cocaine dealer.

In the old days, when I would get a rude email about *Pearls*, I would reply with what looked like a form email thanking the person for their support and informing them that they would now be placed on my mailing list.

65

Panel 1: HEY, GONESOON, HAVE YOU EVER THOUGHT ABOUT MAKING A WILL SO THAT YOUR LOVED ONES WILL KNOW HOW YOU WANT YOUR POSSESSIONS DISTRIBUTED?

Panel 2: THAT'S A GOOD POINT. CAN YOU WRITE THIS DOWN FOR ME? / SURE.

Panel 3: 'ONE CARROT. TO WHOMEVER PICKS IT UP.'

Panel 4: GONESOON HAS AN ANNOYING SENSE OF HUMOR.

I should bring Gonesoon back. He was a good character. And if you send me a rude email saying otherwise, you're going right on the mailing list.

Panel 1: Dear This Week... You have started out very poorly.

Panel 2: Please improve or I shall skip ahead to next week.

Panel 3: LIFE IS NOT A STREAMING SERVICE. / IT WOULD BE A NICE FEATURE.

I don't know about you, but I am such a short-attention-span viewer that when I watch a movie on Netflix, I constantly have to click the little "10 seconds back" button. As a result, no one likes watching movies with me.

Panel 1: I HAVE FATIGUE DUE TO COVID. / OH, NO. I DIDN'T KNOW YOU HAD HAD COVID.

Panel 2: I DIDN'T. / THEN WHAT ARE YOU TALKING ABOUT?

Panel 3: I'M JUST TIRED OF COVID.

Panel 4: I DON'T THINK THAT'S THE SAME. / SICK AND TIRED, IN FACT.

Panel 1: OH, GREAT WISE ASS ON THE HILL... WHY AM I SO UNHAPPY?

Panel 2: YOU, LIKE MANY OTHERS, ARE TOO CONSUMED BY THE DRIVE TO SUCCEED. YOU MUST FILL THAT DRIVE WITH SOMETHING MORE SATISFYING.

Panel 3: I'VE GOT IT. I WILL ROOT FOR OTHERS TO FAIL.

Panel 4: HE KICKED ME OFF THE HILL.

Rat's line in the third panel is a bit too wordy. He should have just said, "I will root for others to fail." Sometimes I don't notice these things until time passes and I get a second look at the strip.

Panel 1: WHAT ARE YOU DOING, PIG? / LOOKING INTO A CRYSTAL BALL TO TRY AND DETERMINE MY FUTURE.

Panel 2: WHAT DO YOU SEE? / CRYSTAL.

Panel 3: GET HELP. / MAYBE I'M CRUSHED BY A CHANDELIER.

Panel 1: WHAT ARE YOU EATING, PIG? / THESE CHOCOLATE CANDIES WITH A TASTY FILLING MADE BY ISLAMIC FUNDAMENTALISTS IN AFGHANISTAN.

Panel 2: WHAT ARE THEY CALLED? / TALIBONBONS.

Panel 3: AMEREECAN HUMOR BAD. / NO, NO. JUST HIS.

I like to think that there's at least one Taliban guy out there who put this on his refrigerator.

I try to read somewhere between 35 and 40 books a year, though lately they are mostly Lonely Planet travel guides.

Panel 1:
HI, GOAT, HOW'S YOUR NEW EXERCISE PLAN? HAVE YOU QUIT YET?

HEY, THE WORD 'QUIT' ISN'T EVEN IN MY VOCABULARY.

Panel 2:
I HAVE A WORD LIKE THAT.

Panel 3:
WHAT?

'SHARING.'

Panel 4:
GOOD TO KNOW.

SHOOT. I SAID IT.

Panel 5:
HEY, GOAT, WHO'S YOUR VERY BEST FRIEND IN THE WHOLE WIDE WORLD?

Panel 6:
I THINK THAT'S SORT OF A QUESTION MOSTLY ASKED BY CHILDREN. AS AN ADULT, I DON'T REALLY THINK THAT WAY.

Panel 7:
I PREFER TO STAY IN THE KIDDIE POOL OF LIFE.

Panel 8:
NOT A BAD WAY TO LIVE, BUDDY.

HEY, DO YOU EAT THE INSIDE OF AN OREO FIRST?

I just traveled to Southeast Asia with a guy I've been best friends with for the last 51 years. Here we are in front of a Buddhist temple in Bangkok:

I should add here that many of the temples there do not allow you to wear shorts and thus they make you buy pants. I pulled mine up really high.

I bet this actually exists somewhere.

John Glynn, the former president of my syndicate, recently helped me out with something. To thank him, I sent him a crate of mayonnaise. I meant it as a joke, but he ate the whole thing.

That's pretty much the life of a cartoonist.

Political humor! I really should have won that Pulitzer Prize.

This strip seemed to resonate with a lot of people. I think we are all starting to wake up to the depressive effects of our phone.

Fun Twinkie Fact: I had a science teacher in high school who took a bite out of the same Twinkie every year, because a Twinkie will apparently last years without spoiling. Either that or he's dead.

When I was a kid, my dad used to buy Neapolitan ice cream. Because I didn't like the strawberry part, I would get a spoon and carefully carve out only the chocolate and vanilla, leaving just the strawberry part for him. When he asked who did it, I would blame it on my cousin Louis.

Speaking of Eurocentric, it is rather amazing that when I was a kid, we were taught that Columbus "discovered" America, as though the people who were already here weren't really people. Even odder, he wasn't even the first European, as the Vikings landed in Newfoundland centuries before him.

AND NOW A MESSAGE FROM THIS COMIC STRIP'S CREATOR, STEPHAN PASTIS...

MOST PEOPLE DON'T KNOW THAT CARTOONISTS HAVE TO SUBMIT THEIR SUNDAY STRIPS WEEKS IN ADVANCE. THAT MAKES IT HARD TO BE TOPICAL.

FOR EXAMPLE, TODAY'S STRIP WAS DRAWN ON JANUARY 8. AND WHEN I DREW IT, I HAD NO IDEA WHAT WOULD BE HAPPENING IN THE WORLD TODAY.

SO PLEASE HELP BY PICKING THE MOST APT PANEL BELOW AND TOSSING THE REST.

OPTION ①

THE PANDEMIC'S OVER AND OUR LIVES CAN RETURN TO NORMAL.

OPTION ②

THE VIRUS IS WORSE THAN EVER AND EVERYTHING IS BAD.

OPTION ③

THINGS ARE OKAY NOW BUT WILL SOON GET WORSE BECAUSE WE'RE STUCK IN AN ENDLESS @#$@# LOOP!!

THANKS FOR YOUR HELP.

PLEASE DON'T PICK ③... PLEASE DON'T PICK ③...

I like that image of me in the first panel. Maybe I should paint it very large on the side of my garage.

75

Input from my wife regarding the comment below the last strip: "I'd shoot you."

Watch me go! A bonus potty joke! And that's what makes your purchase of this book such a solid investment.

The only word better than "philatelist" (a stamp collector) is "numismatist." Bonus *Pearls* points to you if you know what that is. Answer in the next comment.

Nope. I want to build suspense.

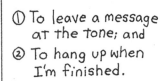

More suspense.

Note from Stephan's editor, Betty Wong: *This is getting tiresome. It's a coin collector. Stephan, can we not do these jokes?*

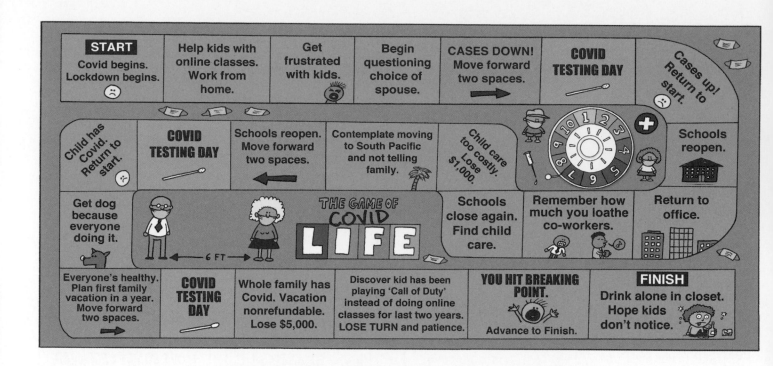

We were one of the families that got a dog during COVID! A springer spaniel named Total. This is her thinking deep thoughts:

I'm one of those people that meticulously keeps a list of every single book I've read. I've heard of some people who do the same thing with movies. But they're weirdos and should be shunned.

This really is what both of my kids do. So I'm cutting them out of my will and using the money to build a spectacular grave for myself. On the side of it will be etched the words, "Should have answered Dad's texts."

 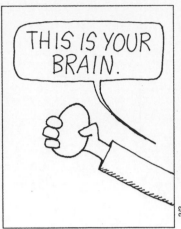  

For those of you who are not as old as me, this was a famous ad in the 1980s. It showed an egg and said, "This is your brain." Then it showed the egg frying and said, "This is your brain on drugs." It always made me hungry.

I was a lawyer for ten years and really didn't like it. But I feel the opposite about cartooning. It never feels like work.

I got an email about this strip from a self-described grammar snob who thanked me for "the reality check of seeing myself described in your strip." Now if I can just fix all the cyclists.

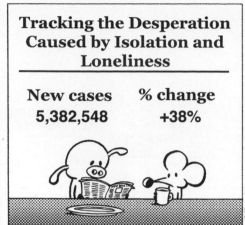

Tracking the Coronavirus

New cases	% change
35,488	-52%

Tracking the Desperation Caused by Isolation and Loneliness

New cases	% change
5,382,548	+38%

CASES ARE RISING.

IF YOU COULD BE ANYONE ELSE, WHO WOULD YOU BE?

A GUY WHO NEVER WANTS TO BE ANYONE ELSE.

PLEASE DON'T INJECT DEPTH INTO MY SHALLOW BANTER.

BRAD PITT.

I've never met Brad Pitt, but I did once meet Matt Damon on the set of a movie in Marseille, France. And by "meet," I mean he walked past me, and I pointed.

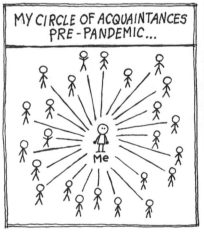

MY CIRCLE OF ACQUAINTANCES PRE-PANDEMIC...

Me

THE CIRCLE OF ACQUAINTANCES I WAS UNFORTUNATELY LIMITED TO DURING THE PANDEMIC...

Me

THE CIRCLE OF ACQUAINTANCES I'M EMBARRASSED TO ADMIT I'M NOW CHOOSING...

Me

PANDEMICS HAVE STRANGE CONSEQUENCES.

NOW I JUST NEED MY DOG AND MY CHEESE.

Aww, this gives me yet another excuse to show my dog Total on the next page, this time licking my ear as a puppy.

82

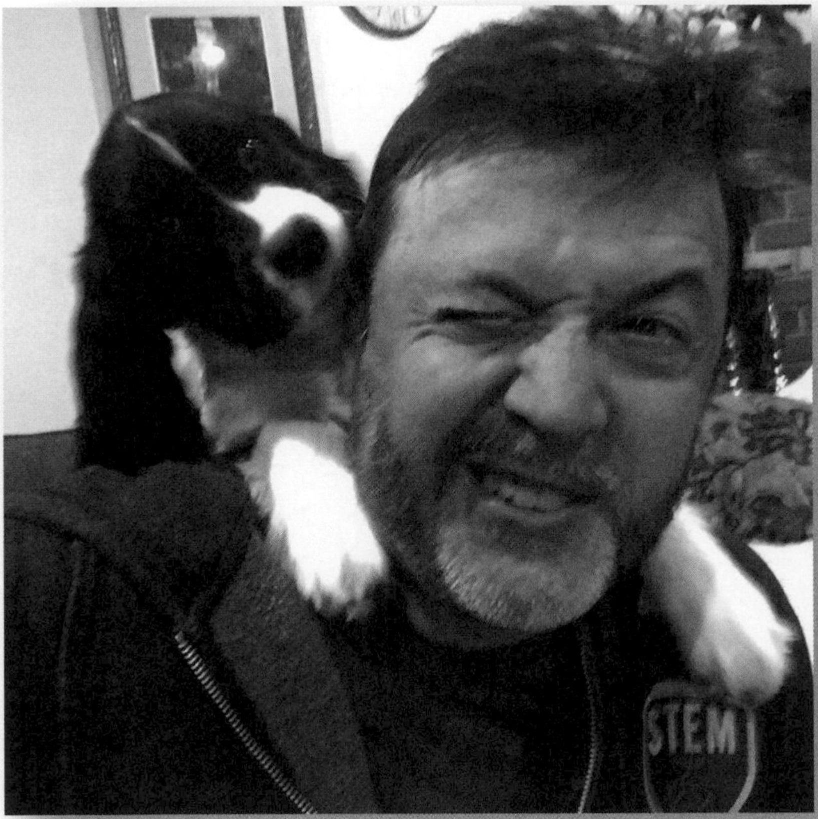
STEM

I have to admit I play Wordle every day. But I don't post my scores because I'm not an annoying peckerhead.

Regarding that last comment: I actually am an annoying peckerhead. But for other reasons.

3/13

"This too shall pass" is always my mother's advice to me. I occasionally draw her in the strip as a gun-toting, beer-guzzling, foul-mouthed chain smoker, which is odd given that she doesn't smoke, swear, drink beer, or have a gun.

WELL, HOWDY-DO AND GOOD MORNING TO YOU, RAT!

WHAT ARE YOU DOING, PIG?

EVERY DAY I TRY TO DO ONE NICE THING FOR OTHERS. THIS WEEK MY NICE THING IS CHEERY MORNING GREETINGS. YOU SHOULD TRY DOING ONE NICE THING A DAY TOO.

THERE. JUST DID IT.

WHAT WAS IT?

DIDN'T PUNCH YOU FOR THAT CHEERY MORNING GREETING.

NON-MORNING PEOPLE SHOULD ALWAYS BE LEFT ALONE.

Whenever I get to my studio in the morning, there's a neighbor who shouts, "Good morning!" as soon as I get out of my car. It always scares the heck out of me.

OH, GREAT WISE ASS, TEACH ME ONE OF LIFE'S TRUISMS.

IN ANY MEETING OF PEOPLE, THERE WILL ALWAYS BE AT LEAST ONE GUY WHO ASKS QUESTIONS ONLY TO DEMONSTRATE HIS OWN KNOWLEDGE TO OTHERS.

IS THAT LIKE WHAT THEY TAUGHT ME ABOUT IN MY GRADUATE THESIS COURSE ON THE GREEK ETHOS OF—

BOOT

JUST MY LUCK I GET THE ONE.

I might be wrong, but I think this is the only time that Goat has gone to the Wise Ass for advice. It's usually either Rat or Pig.

MONDAY WAS TERRIBLE. TUESDAY WAS TERRIBLE. TODAY WAS TERRIBLE.

WELL, TOMORROW IS ANOTHER DAY.

WAY TO BRING ME DOWN.

MEANT TO COMFORT.

ODD LOGIC WHEN DAYS ARE THE PROBLEM.

I've written a number of kids' books, including *Timmy Failure*, *Trubble Town*, and *Looking Up*, and no matter how many times I've done it, I'm always extremely sensitive to comments from the first person who reads it (usually my wife or kids or book agent). Mostly because when you write a book, you've lived alone with it for months, and you don't want to think you've wasted your time on something bad.

Pig is by far the most huggable character in *Pearls*. I think he really balances out the more cynical side of the strip.

The first time I got tested for COVID was at an outdoor testing site here in Santa Rosa, California, and the man who did the test shoved that little stick so far up my nose that it almost came out my ear. At least that's what it felt like.

In early 2022, it felt like the bad news just kept coming.

I've been traveling the United States a lot the past two years, and one of the states I covered from top to bottom was Delaware. I believe it took four hours.

Guard Duck's line in the last panel ("Slava Ukraini") translates to "Glory to Ukraine." After the strip ran, I got a nice message from someone in Ukraine who was at that moment enduring the invasion and wanted me to know how much the strip meant to her. It always amazes me how big of a reach a comic strip can sometimes have.

I almost never engage with someone who insults me or the strip online. And I think that's for two reasons: (1) After this many years, I've heard just about everything, and it usually doesn't affect me; and (2) If I do respond, I've lost, because that's usually what the person wants—my attention.

"Stupidosity" and "smartitude" should both be words. Please use them in your daily speech and make that happen.

I know I've said it before, but I am obsessed with boxes. They have appeared in countless *Pearls* strips. And I honestly believe it's because when I was a toddler, my dad used to bring cardboard boxes home from his liquor store and pull me around in them. Then I would drink all the whiskey that was in them and pass out in my stroller.

I really do think this is the definition of heaven.

Regarding my earlier comment on the "Box O' Redemption" strip: My publisher would like me to inform you that three-year-old me was not actually drinking whiskey.

I've done this before. It changes the meaning of the text rather dramatically.

Panel 1: I RAISED ALL THIS CASH TO FUND A CAMPAIGN AGAINST OUR CURRENT CITY COUNCIL'S DUMB PROPOSALS. WE PUT UP BILLBOARDS THAT JUST SAY, "OH, PULLEASE."

Panel 2: HAVE THEY BEEN A SUCCESS?

NO. THEY'VE HAD NO IMPACT AT ALL. I'M THINKING OF NO LONGER FUNDING IT.

Panel 3: YOU WANT TO DEFUND THE PULLEASE?

Panel 4: SINCE WHEN ARE PUNS A CRIME?

SINCE NOW.

The "defund the police" campaign seemed to inflame everyone's passions in 2020 and 2021. So I thought it would be fun to include it in the strip and make everyone angry all over again.

Panel 1: PARDON ME, BUT I'M WITH 'PEOPLE FOR CONGRESSMAN BOB' AND I'D LIKE TO GIVE YOU THIS PAMPHLET.

Panel 2: ALSO, I LOVE THE LANDSCAPING. NICE, BIG SANDBOX FOR A YARD. YOU MUST HAVE KIDS, WHICH IS GOOD. MEANS YOU CARE ABOUT THE FUTURE.

Panel 3: ALSO, I SEE I'M SINKING. IS THIS BY CHANCE QUICKSAND?

IT IS.

Panel 4: WE'LL DO THIS EVERY ELECTION YEAR.

When my syndicate colored this strip for newspapers (they color all the dailies; I color the Sundays), they goofed and made the sand green, which made the man look like he was sinking inexplicably into grass, thereby confusing just about everyone who read the strip.

Panel 1: HEY, NEIGHBOR BOB...HOW MUCH MONEY DO YOU MAKE?

Panel 2: PIG, NEIGHBOR BOB DOESN'T WANT TO ANSWER A QUESTION LIKE THAT. IT'S NOT POLITE.

OH.

Panel 3: PLEASE, IF YOU WILL, TELL ME HOW MUCH MONEY YOU MAKE, THANK YOU.

Panel 4: STILL DIDN'T ANSWER.

Because of the *Timmy Failure* book series, I have spoken at a lot of grade schools. And invariably, at many of the schools, one of the children would raise their hand and ask, "How much money do you make?" I would usually respond, "More than you, you little turd. Now shut up before I poke you in the eye."

Regarding that fourth panel, on the next page is a photo me in feeding an elephant in Thailand. Sadly, I was almost trampled to death shortly thereafter.

Speaking of refunds, I recently stayed at a hotel in Phoenix, Arizona, where I found a cockroach the size of a small dog in the shower. So I went downstairs and asked for a refund. When the hotel said no, I showed them and all the other guests behind me a photo I had taken of the cockroach. I got the refund.

I'm 55 as of the writing of this commentary. But maturity-wise, I'm 14.

There are so many cool names for groups of animals. For example, a group of tigers is called an ambush. A group of rhinos is called a crash. And a group of ravens is called an unkindness.

People do this all the time at the café where I write. They usually claim the table by putting their stuff on it. One of these days, I'm gonna walk over and push all their crap on the floor and say, "I hope you've learned something from this."

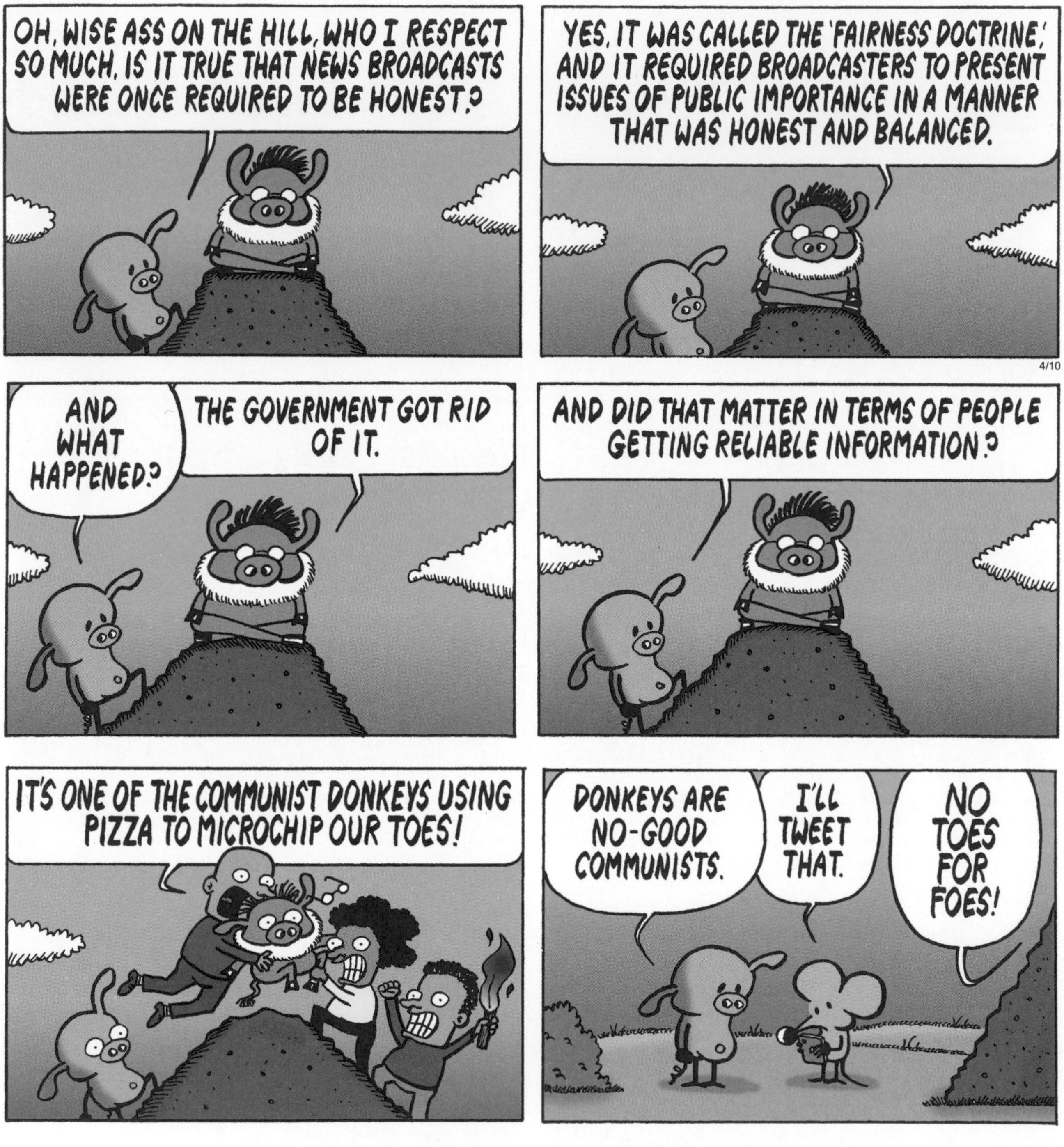
OH, WISE ASS ON THE HILL, WHO I RESPECT SO MUCH, IS IT TRUE THAT NEWS BROADCASTS WERE ONCE REQUIRED TO BE HONEST?
YES, IT WAS CALLED THE 'FAIRNESS DOCTRINE,' AND IT REQUIRED BROADCASTERS TO PRESENT ISSUES OF PUBLIC IMPORTANCE IN A MANNER THAT WAS HONEST AND BALANCED.
4/10
AND WHAT HAPPENED?
THE GOVERNMENT GOT RID OF IT.
AND DID THAT MATTER IN TERMS OF PEOPLE GETTING RELIABLE INFORMATION?
IT'S ONE OF THE COMMUNIST DONKEYS USING PIZZA TO MICROCHIP OUR TOES!
DONKEYS ARE NO-GOOD COMMUNISTS.
I'LL TWEET THAT.
NO TOES FOR FOES!

The guy's line in the fifth panel was a mashup of various conspiracy theories that were floating around at the time. One was that Bill Gates had put a microchip in the COVID vaccine so he could track us (our phones already do a pretty good job of that), and the other was that Hillary Clinton was trafficking children in the basement of a pizza joint.

There was a story a few years back about an employee in a donut shop who did very bad things to the donuts. Never annoy your food server.

HEY, THERE... CLEVER NAME FOR AN ICE CREAM SHOP... I'LL TAKE TWO.

i scream

AHHHHHHHHH AHHHHHHHHH

i scream

THANKS FOR HOLDING MY ICE CREAM.

WE MIGHT HAVE CONFUSED THIS GENTLEMAN.

i scream

I was recently in New Orleans and had the best ice cream cone I've ever had at a place called Parish Parlor on Magazine Street. I'm only saying this because (1) it's true; and (2) I'm hoping one of you shows them this book, and I get a lifetime of free ice cream.

DID YOU LOOK FOR A JOB YESTERDAY?

I WANTED TO, BUT MY DISABILITY FLARED UP.

WHAT'S THE DISABILITY?

SOFITIS.

WHAT IS IT?

AN ABNORMALLY STRONG DESIRE TO LIE ON ONE'S SOFA AND DO NOTHING.

PROBABLY NOT A DISABILITY.

OFTEN ACCOMPANIED BY BEERTOSIS GUZZLEITIS.

I THINK I FIGURED OUT WHAT MY PROBLEM IS.

WHAT'S THAT?

IT'S THAT LIFE IS AN AIRPLANE RIDE.

AND I'M ALWAYS IN BOARDING GROUP 6.

NO OVERHEAD SPACE LEFT FOR YOU.

WHO ARE THESE BOARDING GROUP ONE-STERS?

No matter what I do, I am always in the last boarding group, especially on Southwest Airlines, where I can never remember to check in 24 hours before my flight. I'm only saying this because (1) it's true; and (2) I'm hoping one of you shows them this book and I get a lifetime of free flights.

The band Titus Andronicus incorporates this famous speech into their song, "A More Perfect Union." I listen to it a lot when I write the strip.

Panel 1: WHAT'S THIS STRIP YOU'RE DOING? / WELL, THIS GUY IS MAKING FUN OF THIS HORSE'S WIFE AND SAYING SHE HAS A FUNNY MANE.

Panel 2: SLAP!

Panel 3: KEEP MY WIFE'S MANE OUT YO' @*&#6# MOUTH!

Panel 4: I LIKE THIS TREND.

This was based on Will Smith's now infamous Oscars moment when he slapped Chris Rock and yelled, "Keep my wife's name out yo' #$%#$%@ mouth!" Believe it or not, one large newspaper pulled the strip, telling my editor, "(We) avoid the cursing symbols when it evokes the 'F' word or other very harsh language, and everyone definitely knows what Will Smith said."

Panel 1: I'M NEVER HAPPY. / YOU KNOW, RAT, HAPPINESS IS A CHOICE.

Panel 2: IT IS? / YES.

Panel 3: THEN TELL ME WHO'S BEEN MAKING THOSE CHOICES SO I CAN KICK HIM IN THE REAR.

Panel 4: LET ME START OVER. / NO, SERIOUSLY, GIMME A NAME.

Panel 1: WHAT ARE YOU DOING, PIG? / TRYING TO REMEMBER THE WORD FOR WHEN YOU KEEP UP TO DATE WITH THE NEWS.

Panel 2: ABREAST?

Panel 4: OH, THIS IS MATURE. / CAN WE DO 'ABUT' NEXT?

Remember earlier when I said that maturity-wise, I was about 14 years old? Still applies.

From the Department of Continuity Errors: When I ran this, I totally forgot that just one month earlier I had done a strip where Guard Duck was fighting in Ukraine. Maybe he gave up and came home.

I probably could have gotten away with "hell" in that last panel, as I've done it before. But given what happened with the Will Smith strip, who knows.

Whenever I go on book tours, the most common comment I get from people (other than that I'm handsome and somehow still humble) is that I don't do enough croc/Zebra strips. So I should probably do more of them.

From the Department of I May Actually Be Nutters: I do sometimes walk around my yard and take a moment to talk to the plants, as I've heard that it can have a positive effect. So far, most of them have died.

I was at a diner in New Orleans during COVID when a customer came in, sat in the booth next to me, and purposely began coughing everywhere. The servers ran over, moved me to the other side of the restaurant, and kicked the guy out. It was all very odd.

Regrettably, I actually made a teacher cry one time. It was my tenth-grade chemistry teacher, and I was so obnoxious in class (I never stopped talking) that she took me aside one day after school, asked me to stop, and started crying. I felt really bad, so I stopped entirely. Well, almost entirely.

That's the real statistic as to humans killed by sharks annually. But the real eye opener is the number of sharks killed by humans every year: 100,000,000.

Wise Ass is my most popular new character. He is also my only new character.

I wish I could take credit for noticing this, but it was actually cartoonist Maria Scrivan (*Half Full; Nat Enough*) who told me about it. I asked her if I could use it in the strip and she said yes.

Sadly, this is true. During World War II, the United States took 125,000 Japanese Americans living here in America and put them in concentration camps. Two-thirds of them were United States citizens. It is one of the great injustices in American history.

I've been lucky enough to have a number of careers: lawyer, syndicated cartoonist, kids' book author, and screenwriter. I've enjoyed all but one of them.

Holy smokes—a *ton* of people filled this form out and sent it to my editor, Reed Jackson, who forwarded most of them to me. Fortunately, no one chose, "I wish ill upon Stephan."

I actually drew this strip around three years before it was published, but I kept forgetting to run it during graduation time, and then COVID hit and there were *no* graduations. So I finally ran it in the spring of 2022.

When I was a little kid and had to go on a long car trip with my family, I used to play this game where I stared out the window and imagined a man on skis racing alongside us in the next lane. But he would always crash and die a fiery death.

I just noticed a goof on this one. I meant to say "eulogy" in that first panel, not "obituary." Which is why Pig says, "No one likes a long speech, Bob" in the last panel.

Class Assignment

Please state your hopes for the future.

Was not aware there would be one.

MAYBE I JUST SHOULDN'T ASK THIS GENERATION.

DRINKING MORE IS THE ANSWER, BOB.

Did you hear that, kids? Drinking is always the answer.

HEY, RAT. WHAT'S THAT?

A GET-WELL CARD.

OH, I'M NOT ILL, AND BESIDES, I'M SURPRISED YOU'RE GIVING ME ANYTHING. I THOUGHT YOU'D BE UPSET I TOOK THE LAST OF THE COFFEE WITHOUT MAKING A NEW POT.

OH.

IS A GET-WELL CARD STILL THOUGHTFUL IF YOU'RE THE ONE WHO CAUSED THE HARM?

I LIKE TO THINK SO.

When I was a lawyer, I'd only make a new pot if I heard someone walking toward the breakroom who might catch me taking the last of the coffee. And that's the kind of person you're dealing with here.

HEY, PIG, WHERE WERE YOU TODAY?

BUYING A MODEL TRAIN SET.

I LOVE MODEL TRAINS. WHAT SCALE SIZE? N? O? HO? ONE WITH DIGITAL COMMAND CONTROL?

ONE THAT GOES 'CHOO CHOO.'

I SEE.

I LIKE TO KEEP IT SIMPLE.

WITH ALL THE TIME PEOPLE NOW SPEND CREATING CONSPIRACY THEORIES ONLINE, WE THOUGHT WE'D HELP YOU CREATE YOUR OWN. JUST CUT OUT AN OPTION IN PANEL 'A' AND PAIR IT WITH OPTIONS IN PANELS 'B', 'C', AND 'D' AND YOU'RE READY TO GO!

PANEL 'A'

MEMBERS OF A SHADOW U.S. GOVERNMENT

TECHNOLOGY COMPANIES

RUSSIAN OLIGARCHS

SPACE ALIENS LIVING IN ROSWELL

5/15

PANEL 'B'

ARE COLLECTING DATA ON

NOW CONTROL

WANT NOTHING MORE THAN TO DESTROY

ARE ORCHESTRATING A COUP TO TRY AND TOPPLE

PANEL 'C'

OUR WAY OF LIFE

TOMATO SOUP CANS

ALL THE WORLD'S SQUIRRELS

YOUR MAMA

PANEL 'D'

AND THAT'S JUST THE BEGINNING!

AND IT STARTS AT NOON TOMORROW!

AND THEN WE'RE ALL GONNA DIE!

AND WE'LL ALL BE FORCED TO READ MORE 'PEARLS BEFORE SWINE' COMICS.

NOW I'M MORE SCARED THAN EVER.

AND IF YOU POST IT ONLINE, IT'S AUTOMATICALLY TRUE.

THAT COMICS OPTION REALLY IS FRIGHTENING.

Speaking of conspiracies, I recently met a person who was a key witness in the investigation of John Kennedy's assassination. She was kind enough to talk to me about Lee Harvey Oswald, whom she knew.

I try to run strips like this on a Monday, a time when many people probably feel this way.

My new car does this, and the first time it happened, it scared the bejesus out of me. It's literally as though a ghost has grabbed the steering wheel.

Like everyone, I am completely dependent on Google for searches. But the app of theirs that I *really* use is Google Maps. I research different countries and put pins in every place I find interesting and want to visit. I probably have at least 20,000 pins saved on the app.

I actually try to do this when I get up in the morning. I smile broadly, even if I'm not happy. I don't know if it works, but I sure look frightening doing it.

Regarding the fourth panel, American newspapers had roughly 114,000 newspaper employees as of 2008. Over the next dozen years, 30,000 of those people lost their jobs. So I can't say it enough—subscribe to your local newspaper, or soon you will have no one to investigate and report on what's happening in your town or county or state. And that's a license for people in power to do bad things.

I would comment on this but I'm too afraid.

There were more I could have used, like IN (Indiana), but I couldn't figure out how to fit it IN.

The stupider the joke, the more I laugh.

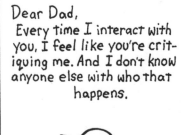

There are many readers who write to me to complain about my incorrect use of "who" and "whom." But I always have to tell them— my characters talk like everyday people talk. If they used "who" and "whom" correctly, they would sound like grammarians, and not themselves.

Like everyone, I waste a crazy amount of time on my phone, particularly in the early morning. I constantly vow to stop, but I never seem to be able to.

Lying to yourself is an underrated skill.

I have absolutely no willpower when it comes to leftover pizza I find in the refrigerator. I will eat all of it. And I will apologize to whomever it belonged to later.

Health Quiz

Alcohol is considered a depressant. Explain why.

BECAUSE WHEN I DRINK, I DEPRESS EVERYONE AROUND ME.

I CAN DO IT SOBER, TOO.

HEY, RAT, I SAW YOUR NEW BOOK CAME OUT. DID YOU SEE THE FIRST REVIEWS ONLINE?

HAHA, NOPE.

WHY NOT?

BECAUSE IF YOU'RE GONNA BE A CREATIVE PERSON, YOU CAN'T PAY ATTENTION TO REVIEWS. YOU JUST FOLLOW YOUR MUSE AND LET THE CHIPS FALL WHERE THEY MAY.

WELL, THAT'S A GREAT WAY TO LOOK AT IT. NOT TO MENTION ADMIRABLE.

THANKS.

I don't know what other authors do, but I never see book reviews unless my agent or editor sends them to me (which I've asked them not to do). I like to remain in my ignorant little bubble.

OH, GREAT WISE ASS, WHAT IS THE SECRET TO LIVING A LONG LIFE?

NOT DYING.

HIS LOGIC IS IMPECCABLE.

Sometimes I like to make the Wise Ass's hill impossibly steep and have Rat defy gravity.

I was recently asked to speak at my own alma mater, the University of California at Berkeley, but I turned it down for fear of saying something that will get me canceled. Ironic, as it was once the home of the Free Speech Movement.

122

I have recently had it pointed out to me that I say "pillow" wrong. I pronounce it "PELL-ow" while other people apparently say it like it's spelled: "PILL-ow." Surely I can't be the only person who says "PELL-ow."

Oh, this is a real pet peeve of mine. Don't say my call is important if you're keeping me on hold for twenty minutes. Also, I'm really hoping most of you say "PELL-ow."

123

This joke is based on the old childhood saying: "Step on a crack, break your mother's back." And the real quote goes on to warn: "Step on a line, break your father's spine." What a wonderful thing for children to recite.

It's amazing to me how many accounts on Twitter seem to be solely for this purpose. All I do on mine is post cute comic strips and make the world a much better place.

Note from my editor Betty Wong regarding that last comment: *A bit arrogant on your part?*

Note from me to my editor Betty Wong regarding her last comment: *Not arrogant enough.*

I was recently called by an investment advisor at the brokerage where I have my account. He was calling to pitch me on some investment product. But I really don't like sales calls and I let him know that. One week later, he sent me a big basket of cheese and fruit to apologize. So it really pays to be unpleasant.

Hullo zeeba neighba. Bad news for you. Crocs now gonna hunt you down and you not know what hit you.

JUST SO YOU KNOW, THAT'S NOT WHAT A DUCK BLIND IS.

Lot of help you was.

When I'm drawing croc strips, I often forget that they speak in lowercase (except for Larry's wife and his son Junior). It's a pain when that happens because I have to rewrite all the dialogue. And that's a real hardship when you're lazy.

THE BEST THINGS IN LIFE ARE FREE!

HEALTH CARE'S NOT FREE. IF YOU DON'T HAVE THAT, YOU JUST GET SICK AND DIE.

THE BEST THINGS IN LIFE ARE FREE!

OH, CRAP. WE'RE HOSED.

I JUST WANT TO BE THE BEST IN THE WORLD AT ONE THING.

I'VE ACHIEVED THAT.

WHAT ARE YOU THE BEST AT?

FORGETTING PEOPLE'S NAMES.

NOT REALLY THE SAME.

GOOD COMEBACK, WHOEVER-YOU-ARE.

Oh, man, this is really me. I forget everybody's names. Even people whose names I've known for years.

I just like the notion of a flamethrower having a "delicate" setting.

I HAD SOME BLOOD WORK DONE AT THE DOCTOR'S OFFICE TODAY.

THAT'S IMPORTANT. DOCTORS CAN REALLY GET A GOOD SENSE OF YOUR OVERALL HEALTH BY ANALYZING WHAT RUNS THROUGH YOUR VEINS.

IT WAS EIGHTY-TWO PERCENT CAFFEINE.

I DON'T THINK THAT'S POSSIBLE.

I AGREE. I THINK IT'S HIGHER.

If I drink caffeinated coffee before I draw, my right hand shakes and makes it hard to draw the strip. So if I know I'm gonna draw, I drink decaf.

WHERE DO YOU GET YOUR NEWS NOW?

I FOLLOW THIS GUY ON TIKTOK.

WHAT'S TIKTOK?

THE SOUND OF THE CLOCK RUNNING OUT ON OUR DEMOCRACY.

IS THAT TRUE?

NO. I WOULD HAVE HEARD ABOUT IT ON TIKTOK.

I very briefly messed around with putting some of my strips on TikTok, but I couldn't figure out how to make the panels appear sequentially and be on the screen for the right amount of time (enough so that people could read each of them). So eventually I gave up and went back to being an old person.

I THINK THE KEY TO MENTAL HEALTH IS TO FORGIVE YOURSELF FOR THE THINGS YOU'VE DONE WRONG IN YOUR LIFE.

THEN GO OUT AND DO MORE WRONG!

I FEEL LIKE YOU'RE EXPLOITING SOMETHING.

NO TIME TO TALK. GOT MORE WRONG TO DO.

I went camping one time in my life—in Boy Scouts, when I was a little kid. During the hike to the campsite, I fell off a log, almost broke my nose, and quit the Boy Scouts the next day.

Okay, now *that's* the steepest Wise Ass hill ever.

HEY, RAT, THIS IS MY COUSIN FROM CHICAGO.

HOW'S IT GOING?

NOT TOO GOOD. I HAVE THIS BAD ROOMMATE BACK HOME NAMED EVAN AND OUR APARTMENT IS RIGHT OVER THE EL.

THE ELEVATED RAILWAY?

YEAH. VERY NOISY. PLUS I MISS MY OLD APARTMENT. MY FAMILY LIVED RIGHT ABOVE ME IN THESE STIES.

6/26

WELL, IF YOU'RE FEELING THAT BAD, YOU SHOULD TRY DRYING DISHES WITH ME. IT'S VERY RELAXING. YOUR MIND DRIFTS AND YOU FEEL BETTER.

THAT'S ALL YOU DO?

YEAH.

IMAGINE THERE'S NO EVAN. IT'S EASY IF YOU DRY. NO EL BELOW US. ABOVE US ONLY STIES.

IMAGINE THERE'S NO STEPHAN.

Believe it or not, it was in Chicago when I was forty-something that I first saw snowfall. I had seen it on the ground before, but I had never seen it fall from the sky. So I took a break from the book signing I was at to go outside and watch it.

I try to put Rat in the first panel in these strips so that he doesn't seem to spring out of nowhere in the fourth panel.

I recently read a book on dinosaurs that explained that most of them were covered with feathers. A little like Big Bird, if Big Bird had sharp teeth and could swallow kids whole.

Patty Norman, my friend from Copperfield's Books (a local chain where I often go to sign books), always prefaces any compliments she gives me with the expression, "I don't want to give you a big head or anything, but . . ."
So I thought I'd turn it into a strip. Also, my head is already big.

It's interesting that Rat gets so much ink on his head, but none on the paper.

I try to go to the gym twice a week to lift weights and run on the treadmill. And when I say "try," I mean I think about doing it but don't.

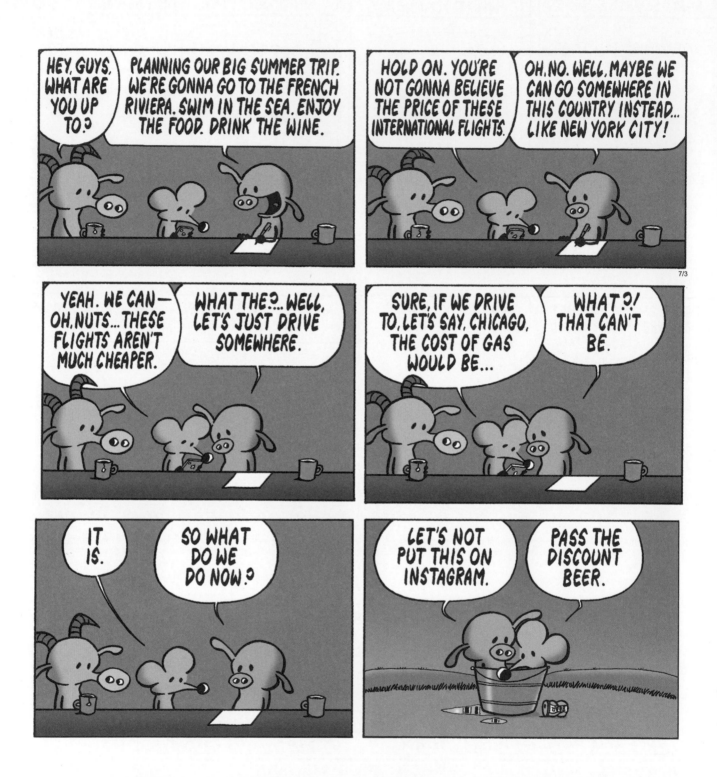

This is a very subtle homage to a 1950s *Peanuts* strip where Charlie Brown sees all of his friends playing in a pool but is not invited to join them. So he goes home and sits in a bucket. Though I don't believe he had a beer.

This would have been funnier if I had put a sad face just below "Too bad you can't find the corner." Too bad I don't think of these things until a year later.

Believe it or not, the closest living descendant of the Tyrannosaurus Rex is the chicken.

I recently did a brain exercise game on my phone and found out I am very deficient when it comes to spatial recognition. So if you take a shape like a cube, and rotate it ninety degrees to the right, my brain blows a fuse.

If you're wondering, I still haven't gotten over the block of mozzarella cheese that went bad in my refrigerator. Grief is a slow process.

True Fact: Almost half of the people who serve in Congress go on to become lobbyists, where they make more than ten times what they made in Congress, raising the question of whether they only served in Congress to one day become rich. Which is probably bad. Unless you're in Congress, in which case it's wonderful.

137

My alarm sound is the song "Total Eclipse of the Heart" by Bonnie Tyler. I can't explain that.

The book Goat is reading is *Dreamland* by Sam Quinones. It's an absolutely stunning story of how a major pharmaceutical company got thousands of Americans hooked on opiates.

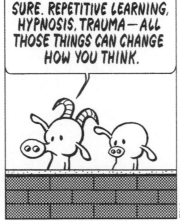

DO YOU THINK IT'S POSSIBLE TO CHANGE YOUR BRAIN?

SURE. REPETITIVE LEARNING, HYPNOSIS, TRAUMA—ALL THOSE THINGS CAN CHANGE HOW YOU THINK.

I MEANT REMOVE YOUR BRAIN AND PLOP IN A NEW ONE.

I DON'T THINK THAT'S A THING.

SCIENCE IS SUCH A LETDOWN.

WHO WAS ON THE PHONE, PIG?

NEIGHBOR BOB. HE'S INVITING US TO A PARTY—OUR THIRD THIS MONTH. LEMME GO TELL RAT.

PLEASE BRING BACK THE LOCKDOWN. PLEASE BRING BACK THE LOCKDOWN. PLEASE BRING BACK THE LOCKDOWN.

I DON'T THINK HE'S GOING.

I don't miss the part of the lockdown that barred travel, but I do miss not having to go to social events.

HEY, GUYS, WHAT ARE YOU UP TO?

JUST TALKING. JOIN US.

WILL THE CONVERSATION BE EXCLUSIVELY ABOUT ME?

PROBABLY NOT.

WHAT A WASTE OF TIME THAT WOULD HAVE BEEN.

I often say that of all the characters in the strip, I'm most like Rat. But as I get older, I think I'm becoming more like Pig. Which means maybe there's hope for me after all.

A very high percentage of the human characters I draw are bald. The deep and profound reason for that is that it's easier to draw than hair.

I have had to stop talking to some acquaintances because they seem especially obsessed with bad news, which always brings me down. I, on the other hand, am an endless fount of joy.

I eat by myself at restaurants all the time. Mostly because I enjoy it. But also because I don't have any friends.

Note regarding that last comment: Fine, I have one friend, Emilio. But he, too, prefers that I eat alone.

In the early days of *Pearls*, I couldn't do this strip, as you generally weren't allowed to mention illegal drugs. But now that marijuana is legal in so many states, it's a closer call.

This comic strip's creator, Stephan Pastis, may or may not have partaken of a now-legalized substance in his home state of California.

The result is this new character who he is calling Spanish-Speaking-Chicken-in-a-Levitating-Frying-Pan, which we now present to you in its unedited form.

— Andrews McMeel Syndication

We apologize for any inconvenience.

I only tried to write the strip one time while high. It didn't work. But I did eat every chip in the house.

142

Meet Bob.

Bob reviews every restaurant he goes to on Yelp.

Please don't give us a bad review.

We'll see.

And every indie album he gets on iTunes.

"ONE STAR... JEJUNE AT BEST."

TYPE TYPE TYPE

7/24

And every place he rents on AirBNB.

"Host did not provide mint on pillow."

And every book he buys on Amazon.

"ONE STAR. A TRAVESTY."

Bob used to be just an average guy.

But now Bob impacts the business of everyone he encounters.

My latte wasn't the exact temperature I asked you for.

Please, Bob. I need this job.

WELCOME TO THE AGE OF BOB.

BWAH HA HAA

DUMB STRIP. ZERO STARS.

THAT'S HARSH, BOB.

I rarely give bad reviews to anything, especially Airbnbs, unless there was something *really* wrong with the place and the owner didn't seem to care. Then the Rat in me comes out. So ignore what I said earlier about my becoming more like Pig.

143

Wise Ass's response here really seems to be the key to success for a lot of people I've known. They always bounce back when something bad happens. I, however, curl into a little ball and weep.

While staying at a hotel in Cambodia recently, I locked my wallet in the little safe that the hotel provides. I chose the code "1234" because I'm pretty sure no thief would ever think of that.

Note regarding my last comment: Apparently, the codes "1234," "1111," and "0000" account for roughly 20 percent of all four-digit passwords. So feel free to steal my wallet.

I am constantly amazed at the number of creative people who go online to read reviews of their work. Even worse, some of them engage with the reviewer or commenter. To me, that seems nutters.

I only knew of Y.A. Tittle (former quarterback of the New York Giants) because of a famous photo of him after a sack where he is down on his knees and dripping blood. Just Google his name, and it will be one of the first photos to pop up. Though maybe don't do it while you're eating breakfast.

OH, GREAT WISE ASS, I AM ALWAYS UNHAPPY AND ANGRY AND NEED TO KNOW IF MY FUTURE HOLDS ANYTHING BETTER.

YES, YOU WILL ACHIEVE EVERY GOAL YOU SET.

BUT WILL BE JUST AS UNHAPPY BECAUSE YOU STILL WON'T UNDERSTAND THAT HAPPINESS COMES FROM THE INSIDE.

I PUSHED HIM OFF THE MOUNTAIN.

HEY, RAT, THIS IS MY FRIEND, ROBERT. HE'S A PROFESSIONAL FILM CRITIC.

WHAT'S IT FEEL LIKE TO HAVE ALL SEVEN BILLION PEOPLE WITH PHONES NOW DOING THE EXACT SAME THING AS YOU?

THAT HURTS.

YOU'RE NOW JUST A SQUIRT GUN IN THE SEA.

The magazine *Sight and Sound* recently did a poll of movie critics who declared that a French film titled *Jeanne Dielman, 23 quai du Commerce, 1080 Bruxelles* was the greatest film of all time. It is three hours of a woman cooking and cleaning. I defy you to get through it.

YOU OFFERING IT?

ASKING FOR IT.

THIS COULD GET CROWDED.

Sitting in a cardboard box is better than watching *Jeanne Dielman, 23 quai du Commerce, 1080 Bruxelles.*

A fiery pit is better than watching *Jeanne Dielman, 23 quai du Commerce, 1080 Bruxelles.*

I recently traveled to Singapore where every morning I had what is more or less the national breakfast there. It's called kaya toast, and it involves dipping a thick piece of toast coated in coconut jam into a bowl of soft-boiled eggs, to which you can then add soy sauce and white pepper. It looks like this:

These are all actual place names. Imagine what it's like when the people there have to fill out address forms.

Rat says all the things we want to say, but can't.

I'm big on using time as efficiently as I can. And one thing that has been great lately is writing while I go for long walks. I just go out on a trail near my studio, walk about three miles, and record any ideas I have on the Voice Memos app on my iPhone. Three miles of walking will usually result in at least one strip.

DID YOU HEAR THIS STORY ABOUT ALL THESE PEOPLE GETTING MONKEYPOX?

OH, SORRY... MONKEYPOX CAN'T BE A THING... I'M ALL OUT OF WORRY SPACE.

COME BACK ANOTHER TIME.

I DIDN'T KNOW THAT WAS AN OPTION.

THE SUBTLETIES OF CARTOONING
TODAY'S LESSON:
TONGUE PLACEMENT!

TONGUE ABOVE MOUTH:
SATISFYING MEAL

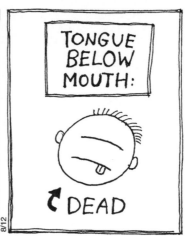

TONGUE BELOW MOUTH:
DEAD

IT'S THE LITTLE THINGS.

WILL KEEP TONGUE UP ALWAYS.

Do people really stick their tongue out like that when they die or is that only in cartoons?

Dear Powers That Be In The Universe...

Lately, I've had so many setbacks that I had to check my calendar.

Is it 'PICK ON ME' month?

THEY RARELY TELL YOU.

I have Pig write to the "Powers That Be In The Universe" instead of to God, because if I mention God, it will result in a number of letters or emails from people who want to tell me about God and how I should pray to him and how I should lead my life. And dammit, I'm perfect already.

152

And now, as a public service, Pearls Before Swine takes a break from its regular comic strip fare to bring you a special message.

HI. I'M CHARLIE, C.E.O. OF A LARGE COMPANY THAT SELLS YOU EVERYDAY HOUSEHOLD GOODS.

IF YOU'RE LIKE THE REST OF US, YOU'RE PROBABLY CONCERNED ABOUT INCREASED PRICES. WE DON'T LIKE THEM ANY MORE THAN YOU DO.

8/14

BUT SADLY, THOSE PRICES BECAME NECESSARY DUE TO COVID-19, SUPPLY CHAIN ISSUES, AND LABOR SHORTAGES, ALL OF WHICH RESULTED IN HIGHER COSTS FOR US.

BUT WHEN YOU PASSED ON THOSE COSTS TO US, YOU ADDED ON ADDITIONAL INCREASES THAT MADE YOUR PROFITS THE HIGHEST THEY'VE BEEN IN YEARS.

WHY YOU LOUSY RAT PUNK @#

NIX THE COMIC... NIX THE COMIC...

I SPEAK TRUTH TO

REPLACE IT... REPLACE IT...

THAT RAT IS WORSE THAN MONDAYS.

Apologies to the great Jim Davis

I got a nice email from Jim Davis on the morning that this strip ran thanking me for the mention.

The deeper question here is how the man's glasses stayed on his face without a nose.

I used to be so afraid of dogs because I was bitten a few times as a kid. But after having two springer spaniels, Edee and Total, I now absolutely love dogs. So this might be a good time to list some of Total's nicknames: Totes, Totes Schmotes, Total Schmodle, Totes McGee, Totes McGibbons, Mr. McGibbons, and perhaps the oddest one of all, Eduardo Valverde.

Speaking of good bars, I was recently at a famous watering hole in Little Rock, Arkansas called White Water Tavern, where Bill Clinton used to hang out. But if the former president went there now, he would see this on the bathroom wall:

AND NOW A MESSAGE FROM DR. RAT, NOTED ANTHROPOLOGIST AND RESIDENT GENIUS...

I HAVE RECENTLY COMPLETED AN EXHAUSTIVE STUDY AND HAVE DETERMINED THAT 50% OF ALL PEOPLE ARE MORONS.

SO WHEREVER YOU ARE, LOOK AT THE PERSONS ON YOUR LEFT AND RIGHT. ONE OF THEM IS A MORON.

8/19

SO FAR, VERY ACCURATE.

RIGHT BACK ATCHA.

WHAT ARE YOU LOOKING AT?

REAL ESTATE LISTINGS. I'M LOOKING FOR A SAFE NEIGHBORHOOD TO LIVE.

IN MY NEIGHBORHOOD, WE DON'T EVEN LOCK THE DOORS.

IT'S THAT SAFE?

8/20

THEY STOLE THE DOORS.

I'LL KEEP LOOKING.

OTHERWISE, IT'S PRETTY SAFE.

8/21

I did this strip knowing full well that I am one of the people who spends all day sitting in a café.
But I *am* writing the strip, so technically I'm "working."

Interesting-but-Kind-of-Gruesome Scar Story: When I was a little boy, I was absentmindedly sawing a cardboard aspirin package with a steak knife (hey, this was before video games) when the knife slipped and sliced deeply into my left hand. The scar is still visible.

Someone (I don't know who) has taken the time to write a massive entry for *Pearls Before Swine* on Wikipedia, complete with names, dates, and citations. Whoever did it knows more about the strip than I do.

SO I GET A GREAT DEAL ON TOILET PAPER AT THE GROCERY STORE AND I TAKE IT HOME.

THAT'S WHEN I NOTICE IT'S NOT TWO-PLY. IT'S ONE-PLY. SO NOW I HAVE TO USE TWICE AS MUCH TOILET PAPER. WHICH IS NO BARGAIN AT ALL.

AND THAT'S WHY I HATE MANKIND.

BIG LEAP THERE.

WHAT MONSTER HATH WROUGHT THIS INJUSTICE UPON ME?

This happened to me, and it was very traumatic. I now read the toilet paper package very carefully before purchase.

WHAT ARE YOU DOING, PIG?

I REALIZED THAT EVERYONE WANTS TO WIN IN LIFE. BUT THAT MEANS SOMEONE ALWAYS HAS TO LOSE. WHICH MAKES PEOPLE SAD.

WILL LOSE FOR YOUR BENEFIT

SO INSTEAD, I'LL DO ALL THE LOSING. SO HERE'S YOUR TROPHY. YOU CAN FILL IN WHATEVER IT IS YOU BEAT ME AT.

WILL LOSE FOR YOUR BENEFIT

THAT CAN'T FEEL GOOD.

SAYS THE GUY NOT DOMINATING LIFE.

This is another strip that I think was loosely inspired by a *Peanuts* comic where Linus goes into great detail telling Charlie Brown all about an exciting win for his football team, after which Charlie Brown simply asks, "How'd the other team feel?"

Whuh you doing, son?

VOCAB QUIZ.

Use the following word in a sentence:

doctorate

The fat doctorate too much and hurt his tummy.

THANKS FOR THAT.

Good wordisms is my specialness.

I watched all of Christopher Nolan's film, *Dunkirk*, without once realizing that the movie jumped around in time.

In a four-panel strip, the pause in the third panel is a good device if you use it correctly. It needs to be a moment where the character is realizing something. It is yet another thing I learned from reading *Peanuts* comics.

I have never attended any of my high school reunions, mostly because I fear seeing how my classmates have aged, which means I've aged as well. And I'm pretty sure I haven't aged.

Captain Tony's Saloon is a famous bar in Key West, Florida where Ernest Hemingway frequently drank. It has a large tree trunk right in the middle of the bar from which pirates were hanged.

When we filmed *Timmy Failure* in Portland, Oregon, we incorporated a hand-painted quote we found on a wall that said, "Long live the wildcards, misfits and dabblers."

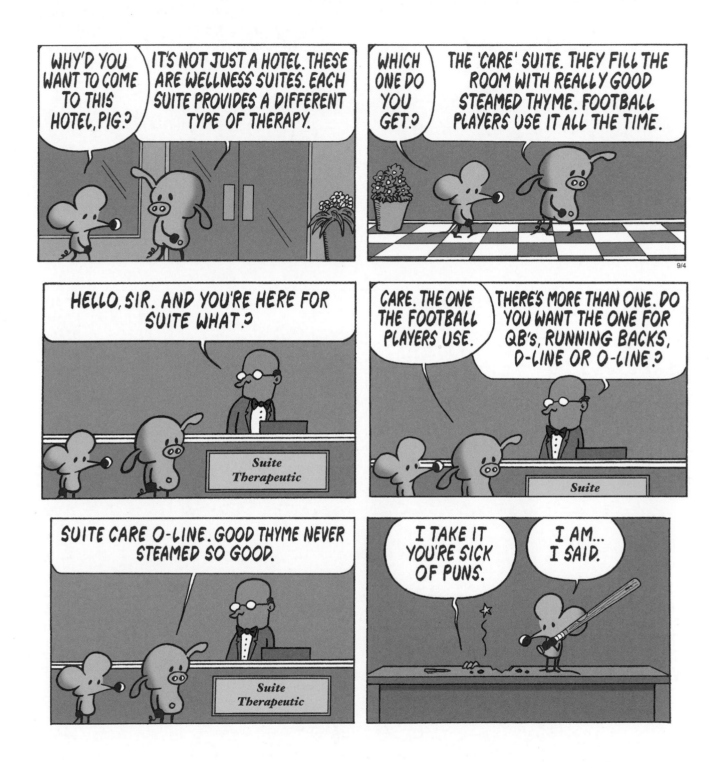

This was a popular strip, at least for people who like elaborate puns. For the rest of the population, not so much.

WELL, THE BANK CALLED...

WE GOT THE LOAN!!

YOU GUYS GETTING A HOUSE?

THIS WEEK'S GROCERIES.

OH.

THEY DID PUT A LIEN ON OUR POP-TARTS.

This strip was in response to a huge surge in grocery prices that occurred in June of 2022.

RAT'S WORD O' THE DAY:

WORRYBOMB

THE BURST OF WORRY THAT GOES OFF IN YOUR HEAD AT THE EXACT MOMENT YOU TRY TO SLEEP.

KABOOM

NO KNOWN CURE.

CAN A BRAIN BE DEFUSED?

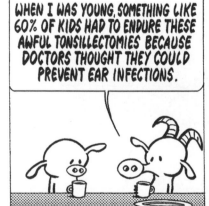

WHEN I WAS YOUNG, SOMETHING LIKE 60% OF KIDS HAD TO ENDURE THESE AWFUL TONSILLECTOMIES BECAUSE DOCTORS THOUGHT THEY COULD PREVENT EAR INFECTIONS.

REALLY?

YEP. TURNS OUT IT WAS SOMETHING WE DIDN'T NEED THAT NOBODY LIKED.

YOU GUYS TALKING ABOUT FACEBOOK?

ONE INVASIVE PROCEDURE AT A TIME PLEASE.

I CAN'T EVEN REMOVE THAT FROM MY PHONE.

I've deleted Facebook from my phone twice, only to then put it back on.

164

The truth is I rarely use a television anymore. If I want to watch something, I generally watch it on my phone.

I drew this strip in the year before COVID, and when COVID hit, it felt like an odd time to run it. For one thing, it made light of disease at a time when many people were dying of the virus. And for another, no one was using communal tables, much less going into cafés. So I didn't run it until almost three years later.

A lot of people were moved by this strip, and by Pig's comforting of a man who had lost a loved one. Without realizing it, I ran it on the anniversary of 9/11.

I love my simple little morning routine. I sit on the patio of my studio and have coffee and a bagel. Below is my view.

167

"Can we all get along?" was the question posed by Rodney King during the 1992 riots in Los Angeles. I was at UCLA Law School at the time and had to get a pass to walk to and from campus during what was a city-wide curfew.

Beep
Boop
Beep
Beep
Boop
Boop
Beep

Thank you for calling Bombast cable. Your approximate wait time is....

...So long you'll want to punch us in the face.

9/15

AT LEAST THAT'S AN ACCURATE ESTIMATE.

My wife Staci periodically calls the cable company and tells them we're canceling. Then they lower our monthly charge. She's very smart that way.

OH, GREAT WISE ASS, ARIZONA IS ABBREVIATED TO 'AZ' BECAUSE 'AR' WAS ALREADY TAKEN BY ARKANSAS. AND ALASKA IS 'AK' BECAUSE 'AL' WAS ALREADY TAKEN BY ALABAMA. SO WHY...

...IS HAWAII 'HI' WHEN 'HA' WAS PERFECTLY AVAILABLE? YES!

BECAUSE HAWAII IS MESSING WITH US.

9/16

YOU'D THINK A STATE THAT NICE WOULD BE KINDER.

Hawaii is one of the few states where I have not yet done a book signing, mostly because I've always assumed there are much better things to do in Hawaii than go to my book signing. Heck, if I was in Hawaii, *I* wouldn't go to my book signing.

HEY, RAT. WHAT'S ALL THIS?

The moment

I'M LIVING LIFE IN THE MOMENT.

The moment

9/17

SOME THINGS ARE SO OVERRATED.

The moment

I am convinced that people who are a bit over-the-top with political signs and bumper stickers are unhappy with some aspect of themselves and are compensating by projecting that outward toward external things. And if you are one of those people, I take all of that back.

Goat looks very awkward when he smiles.

My life's precious moments are spent in a much more important endeavor—playing Boggle With Friends on my phone. It involves a 16-letter board where you make as many words as you can in two minutes. I think I'm addicted to it.

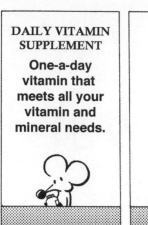

DAILY VITAMIN SUPPLEMENT

One-a-day vitamin that meets all your vitamin and mineral needs.

SHAKE
SHAKE
SHAKE

GLUG
GLUG
GLUG
GLUG

VITAMINS SHOULDN'T COME IN GUMMY BEAR SHAPES.

WE'LL NEED TO PUMP YOUR STOMACH.

Speaking of addictions, I have recently started eating Tums like candy, though I think they're an antacid and not a dessert. So if you ever hear in the news that I've overdosed on Tums, you should probably believe it.

WHAT ARE YOU DOING, RAT?

I'M WAITING TO BE DISCOVERED FOR THE BRILLIANT GENIUS I AM.

HOW WILL THAT HAPPEN?

SOMEONE WILL JUST WALK BY AND SAY, "HEY, YOU, YOU'RE A GENIUS AND DESERVE BETTER IN LIFE."

NOT SURE IT WORKS THAT WAY.

NOT WITH YOU BLOCKING HIS VIEW.

DO YOU HAVE A MORAL CODE YOU LIKE TO LIVE BY?

I DO.

WHAT IS IT?

CRUSH ALL WHO GET IN MY WAY.

NOT SURE THAT'S A MORAL CODE.

IT'S THE CLOSEST I GET.

I try to crush the will of my opponents in Boggle With Friends. All while chewing Tums.

TODAY I, RAT, ANNOUNCE MY CANDIDACY FOR THE UNITED STATES SENATE.

I AM RUNNING FOR THE SAME REASONS MOST SENATORS DO... TO BE RICH AND POWERFUL. BUT MOSTLY TO BE RICH.

FOR ON A SALARY OF $174,000, MANY SENATORS SOMEHOW LEAVE OFFICE WITH TENS OF MILLIONS OF DOLLARS.

HOW DOES THIS HAPPEN? *LEGALLY.* TEE HEE HEE SORRY, SHOULDN'T HAVE GIGGLED IN THAT PART.

FINALLY, I PROMISE YOU THIS—IF I CAN EVER DO SOMETHING IN OFFICE THAT BENEFITS ME GREATLY WHILE SOMEHOW HELPING YOU IN SOME SMALL, INCONSEQUENTIAL WAY, I WILL DO IT.

WHY? BECAUSE I CAN'T BE ELECTED WITHOUT YOU. WHICH IS WHY I'M CALLING MY CAMPAIGN THE 'ON-THE-HEADS-OF-THE-PEASANTS EXPRESS.'

AT LEAST HE'S HONEST.

OKAY, THIS PEASANT IS WIGGLING TOO MUCH. CAN I GET A NEW PEASANT?

Speaking of that second-to-last panel, I recently saw a video on Instagram of a toddler who stands on the back of his puppy to steal snacks off the kitchen counter. Proving that you can't trust anyone.

There is a Buddhist temple in Tokyo where you randomly draw a stick that contains your fortune. But if you get a bad one, you just put it back and take another. I wish life worked that way.

I am eagerly awaiting the day when Starbucks gives up on its pompous, confusing names for cup sizes (tall, grande, venti). Because the "tall" is not the tall one. The "grande" is not the large one. And nobody knows what the &$%# "venti" means.

When I can't sleep, I just watch travel shows on my phone. The one flaw in the system is that when I finally do fall asleep, I drop the phone onto the bridge of my nose.

Speaking of lost items, when I was a little kid, my godmother in Pittsburgh gave me a program from the 1909 World Series between the Pirates and the Tigers. To this day I have no idea today where it is. It's probably the most valuable thing I've ever lost.

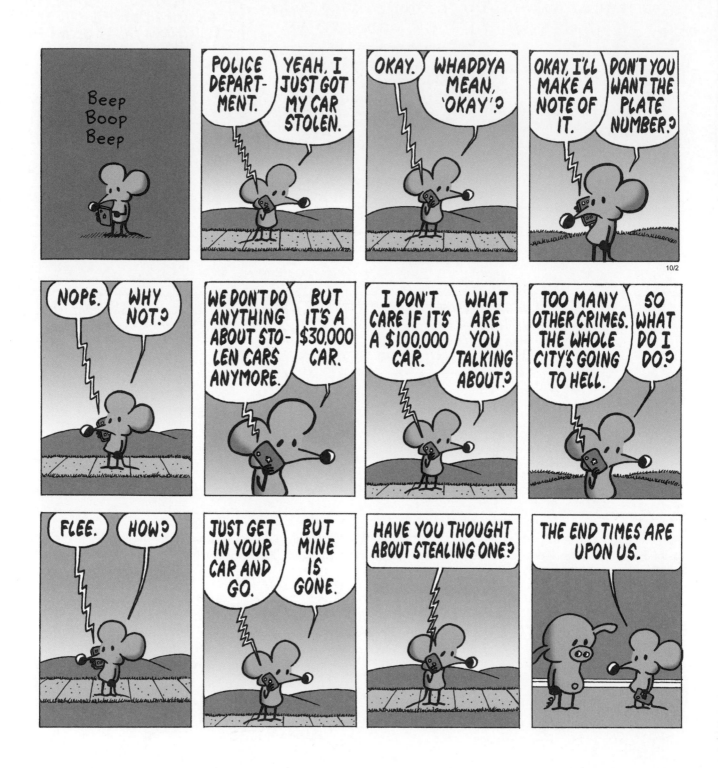

I did this strip after my niece in Southern California had her car stolen and the police told her there was nothing they could do about it.

When I was born, my father's gender reveal party for me was to call his buddy and say, "We had a boy."

I am so uncomfortable at parties that I will frequently find a chair that is far away from everyone else and sit there by myself. Which inevitably attracts people who walk over and start talking to me. And all I can think in those moments is, "What do you think this is—a social event?"

177

For reasons I can't explain, Wise Ass's head gets significantly larger in that last panel. Too bad I only notice these things years later.

No one who's ever told me, "Let's catch up soon," has ever caught up with me soon.

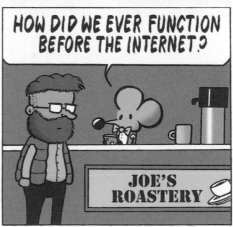

In strips like this, it's important that Rat not seem *too* unlikable. So I try and make the customer even *more* unlikable. And the best way to do that is to make them a hipster.

Note regarding that last comment: You can always make fun of annoying hipsters because nobody who's an annoying hipster would ever call themselves an annoying hipster.

This strip triggered some odd reactions about what exactly was wrong with this guy's drink order. To me, it's just a bit snooty and entitled. Which I guess offended some people who are snooty and entitled.

Depression is something I have fought for years. It usually comes out of nowhere. I get through it by remembering that it generally lasts no more than twenty-four hours.

Have I mentioned I like graves? On the next page is Lucille Ball's, in Jamestown, New York.

 DO YOU THINK IT'S POSSIBLE THAT MOST MEDIA OUTLETS WE FOLLOW ON OUR PHONE OR WHEREVER ARE JUST TOO NEGATIVE?

 AND THAT WE TAKE OUR CUE FROM THEM AND MISS OUT ON ALL THE GOOD THINGS IN THE WORLD?

 GOOD THINGS? THERE ARE GOOD THINGS IN THE WORLD?

 I THINK IT'S POSSIBLE.

10/15

For the record, I have never seen one minute of *Yellowstone*. But I have gone through all of *The Sopranos* series twice.

Someone recently informed me that the Scottish have a term for the act of staying in bed too long, which is to "hurkle-durkle." I'm gonna put that in a strip as soon as I stop hurkle-durkling.

One time when I was really down, I went and sat in our yard. Our dog Total saw me, walked outside, and just laid by my side. Dogs are the best.

Every day I walk this quiet creekside trail near my studio, which is super peaceful and nice until this hipster guy whips by me on an electric bike that must be going at least thirty miles an hour. I'm hoping one day he flies off into the creek.

I think the basic idea behind mindfulness is giving all your attention to the thing that you're doing. So when you're walking by the creek, focus on walking by the creek, and not on the electric bike flying into it.

Whenever I draw birds in the sky, there are always two of them. Never one. Never three. Always two. And it's consistency like that which makes me the beloved cartoonist I am today.

While most self-involved whining on Twitter is just that, I think the guy with his head on fire in the first panel has a legitimate gripe.

If you got this book you're now holding as a present, please don't return it. I've worked very hard on it and if I found it out, I'd probably show up at your front door in tears.

Regarding that last comment about showing up at someone's front door: I once got an email from a guy in my hometown of Santa Rosa saying that he was looking to buy a signed copy of one of my strips for his spouse. I replied that I actually lived in his town and could just drop it off. Which I did, thinking he'd find it pretty cool. Oddly, he didn't really seem to care. So remember, kids: Never do nice things.

I've been told that the reason many restaurants do this is to direct you to their bar, where you'll hopefully buy drinks. Which I do. I'm kind of a moron that way.

My wife just read that last comment and said, "You're a moron in more ways than that."

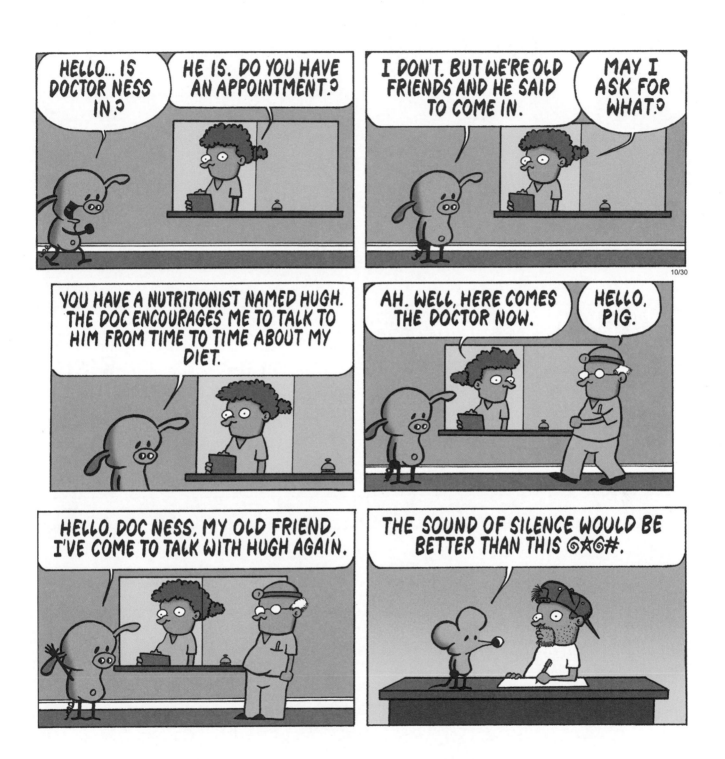

"Hello darkness, my old friend," has to be one of the greatest song openings ever written.

So the joke here is that the word "mares" sounds an awful lot like "mayors," which is how Pig hears it. If only I could sit by each and every newspaper reader and explain all of my jokes.

Anecdote tangentially related to booing: I recently went to a comedy show in Austin, Texas, and sat in the front row with cartoonist Scott Hilburn (*Argyle Sweater*) and the former head of my syndicate, John Glynn. While we didn't boo, we didn't laugh either, as we just didn't find the jokes funny. Finally, one of the comics walked toward us and yelled, "CAN'T YOU GIVE ME ONE F****** LAUGH?" Ironically, it was the one thing that made us laugh.

Pearls Trivia You Maybe Didn't Need That I'm Gonna Tell You Anyway: If Rat is holding a drink, it's either a beer or coffee. For Goat, it's generally tea (as shown by the string of the tea bag) or wine. And for Pig, it's coffee or a soda, but rarely alcohol, as I kind of think of him as a little kid.

MY APPROACH TO THE DAY AHEAD OF ME...

I CAN DO IT!
I CAN DO IT!
I CAN DO IT!

BED IS ALWAYS AN OPTION.

ZZZZZZz

I think someone I know may have just cut-and-pasted the art in the third panel and put it in the fourth panel. It's laziness like that that makes me ill.

TODAY'S AFFIRMATION:
I am not responsible for other people's happiness.

GOOD FOR YOU, RAT. THAT'S AN IMPORTANT REALIZATION.

I did, however, cause their sadness.

NOT WHERE I THOUGHT THAT WAS GOING.

IT'S SORT OF A SPECIAL SKILL.

HOW DO YOU MANAGE TO ALWAYS BE SO NICE TO OTHERS, PIG?

BECAUSE I WANT TO GO TO HEAVEN WHEN I DIE.

AND WHAT DO YOU THINK HEAVEN IS?

HEAVEN IS ONE BIG PANTRY FILLED WITH CHOCOLATE AND CHEESE WHERE YOU CAN EAT AS MUCH AS YOU WANT BECAUSE YOU CAN'T DIE TWICE.

I MAY START BEING GOOD.

Our dog Total sometimes sneaks into our walk-in pantry. Then the door shuts behind her and she gets stuck in there. She'd be a terrible burglar.

Dear Powers-That-Be in-the-Universe...

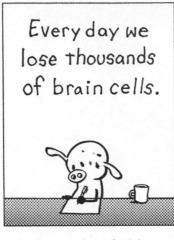

Every day we lose thousands of brain cells.

So why am I not losing weight?

I NEED ANSWERS.

My current weight is 196 pounds. Maybe you don't find that interesting, but let's see you try to fill an entire book with commentary.

WHEN I GO OTHER PLACES AND WALK AROUND, I SEE A LOT OF THINGS THAT ARE REALLY GREAT.

BUT IF YOU LOOK ON SOCIAL MEDIA, THEY SOMEHOW MAKE EVERYTHING SEEM BAD, BAD, BAD. IT'S LIKE THIS DISTORTED VERSION OF REALITY.

THINK OF SOCIAL MEDIA AS A FUNHOUSE MIRROR, BUT WITHOUT THE FUN.

I NEED TO GO TO A DIFFERENT CARNIVAL.

THIS ONE'S MORE OF A HOUSE OF HORRORS.

I'VE BEEN SO UNHAPPY LATELY.

OF COURSE YOU'VE BEEN. IT'S ALL ABOUT THAT FAMOUS QUOTE BY HENRY DAVID THOREAU.

WHAT'S THAT?

'THE MASS OF NON-CYCLISTS LEAD LIVES OF QUIET DESPERATION.'

I THINK YOU CHANGED SOMETHING.

DON'T MAKE ME GO ALL 'UNCIVIL DISOBEDIENCE' ON YOUR @##.

The real Thoreau quote is, "The mass of men lead lives of quiet desperation." He does not mention cyclists.

Booze is fun, kids! And don't let your parents tell you different.

Note from Betty Wong, Stephan's book editor, regarding the last comment: *Children should not drink alcohol.*

I totally goofed and did almost this same joke just ten days earlier. I should ease up on the drinking.

While I don't watch a lot of movies, I'm a sucker for documentaries. My favorite ever is called *Searching for Sugar Man*. It's one of the greatest, most unlikely, stories you'll ever watch.

In 2021, there was a gender reveal party in California that used a pyrotechnic device and inadvertently started a fire that burned 23,000 acres. Surprise!

197

In the early years of *Pearls*, I would have said that Rat was the heart and soul of the strip. But as I've gotten older, I think it's becoming Pig.

I listen to a ton of podcasts as I draw. My favorite is a sports one called *The Bill Simmons Podcast*, but I also listen to *WTF with Marc Maron*, *The Joe Rogan Experience*, *All Songs Considered*, *This American Life*, *Club Random with Bill Maher*, and *The Daily* by the *New York Times*.

I managed to sneak in shout-outs to both my college (U.C. Berkeley) and my law school (UCLA). And while I did not attend Georgetown, I did go there once to see the nearby stairs where the priest in *The Exorcist* falls to his death.

IT'S THE MIDDLE OF THE NIGHT. WHAT ARE YOU STILL DOING UP?

CAN'T SLEEP. WORRIED ABOUT EVERYTHING.

HEALTH? MONEY? RELATIONSHIPS?

THERE ARE 450,000,000 TURKEYS IN THE WORLD. WHAT IF THEY ALL TURNED ON US?

I've never been attacked by a turkey, but I was once accosted by a swan. I ran all the way back to my car.

WELL, GUYS, I'M OFF TO ENJOY A RELAXING VACATION TO REVIVE THE SOUL AND LIFT MY SPIRITS!

WHERE ARE YOU GOING? YOU DON'T EVEN HAVE LUGGAGE.

I'M JUST GETTING OFF SOCIAL MEDIA FOR AN HOUR.

I DIDN'T KNOW THAT WAS AN OPTION.

WHO DO YOU THINK ARE THE GREATEST FICTIONAL CHARACTERS OF THE TWENTIETH CENTURY?

WELL, YOU HAVE HOLDEN CAULFIELD, JAY GATSBY, SHERLOCK HOLMES, SCARLETT O'HARA, ATTICUS FINCH... HARD TO THINK OF MANY WITH A BIGGER IMPACT.

Nov. 26, 1922

GOOD GRIEF. WHO'S THE SAD KID?

THAT CAN'T BE GOOD FOR YOUR BACK.

I ran this strip on what would have been the 100th birthday of *Peanuts* creator Charles Schulz, who I was lucky enough to meet in 1996 at his ice arena in Santa Rosa. On the next page is a photo of the two of us together:

200

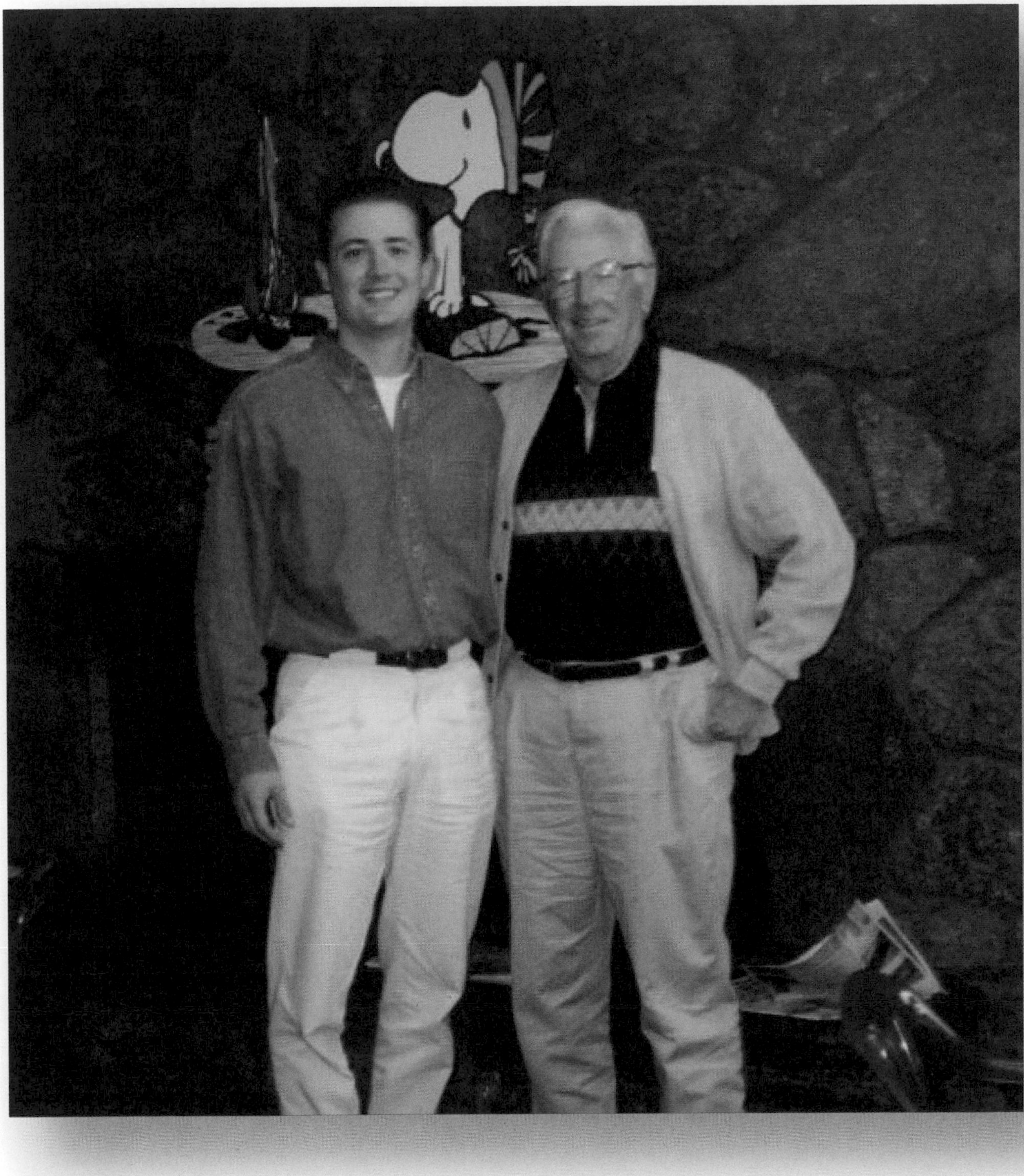

In a crazy coincidence, just one day after my Schulz tribute, I ran this Sunday strip where I colored the pot to look like Charlie Brown's shirt. I didn't notice that detail when I set the strip to run on this day.

I drew this strip after Elon Musk bought Twitter and tried to charge every user $8 a month to have a verified account. Like most people, I did not pay, and lost my verified status. My Twitter account is @stephanpastis.

I made sure to post these strips on Twitter. Whether or not Elon ever saw them, I don't know.

Exercise Goal for the Week

Go to the gym.

Exercise Goal for the Week

✓ Go to the gym.

Exercise Goal for Next Week

Actually go inside it.

I'M MAKING REAL PROGRESS.

WHAT DO YOU DO WHEN AN ANGRY DRIVER AGGRESSIVELY CUTS YOU OFF? SWEAR AT THEM? MAKE A RUDE GESTURE? CUT THEM OFF IN RETURN?

I TRY TO FOCUS ON WHAT MUST BE HAPPENING IN THEIR LIFE TO MAKE THEM SO HOSTILE AND UNHAPPY.

MAYBE YOU'RE NOT UNDERSTANDING.

NO, BUT I'M TRYING TO BE.

When I know I've done something to irritate another driver, I make a point not to look at them. That way, I don't know whether or not they're flipping me off and can instead imagine them smiling and waving.

WHAT ARE YOU DOING, GOAT?

USING TINDER TO FIND A DATE. DO YOU EVER USE IT?

NO. I DON'T WANT TO RISK MEETING ANYONE WHO MIGHT DISAGREE WITH MY OPINIONS OR CHALLENGE MY BELIEFS.

SO I USE 'FIND A TOADY.' IT'S AN APP THAT MATCHES YOU WITH SOMEONE WHO WILL AGREE WITH EVERYTHING YOU THINK OR SAY.

YOU NEED HELP.

YOU'D MAKE A VERY BAD TOADY.

I wrote this strip after talking to a woman who had cut short a number of dates because the men did not agree with her politically.

My local paper is the *Press Democrat* in Santa Rosa, California. I know the editor, Rick Green, and sometimes drop in to see him. When he's not there, I take his candy and hope he blames an intern.

I am of the belief that only pepperoni should be put on a pizza. Okay, fine, maybe sausage and ham as well. But I draw the line at vegetables, which I view as a gross abomination.

When I was a little kid, I got to make two trips to visit my godparents in Pittsburgh. This was in the heyday of the Terry Bradshaw/Franco Harris Steelers and so my room at home was covered with their pennants and posters.

My wife's Toyota has one of these. I always forget and try to shut the trunk manually. And she always says, "You just push the stupid button, you moron."

My wife would like me to clarify that last comment: She has never called me a moron. She only *thinks* it.

When I was a little kid, I would always go to a pizza place in San Marino, California, called Tony's Pizza. They had this deal called the Student Special, which consisted of two slices of pizza and a Coke for just a couple of dollars. The restaurant is still there today. I'm mentioning it in the hope that when I return, I will be handed copious amounts of free pizza.

Every year my wife Staci puts together a very nice Christmas card filled with photos. Usually of our dog. Though one time I believe there was a small photo of me with the caption, "He lives here, too."

Speaking of trivia, *Pearls* was recently a question on Jeopardy. Fortunately, I knew the answer.

CHARACTERS IN THIS CURRENT STRIP INCLUDE AN ARROGANT RAT, A HUMBLE DIMWITTED PIG & A DUCK WHO GUARDS THE PIG'S FRONT LAWN

Elon purchased Twitter for $44 billion, which is appearing more and more like it will go down as one of the biggest business blunders of all time.

Speaking of losing a buck on a rash decision, I was once with a guy at a Jell-O shots bar who was flirting with the female server. She told him that if he just bought the rest of her tray of Jell-O shots, she could leave work and hang out with him. So he bought the entire tray for $75, after which she said she had to go change out of her work clothes. She left and never came back.

Dear life,
You are filled
with too many
horrible
surprises.

So I have a
suggestion.

How 'bout you run
each of these events
by me first and
I'll let you know
if they're a go.

THIS WILL BE A NICE
CHECK ON THE SYSTEM.

DID YOU SEE THE WARRIORS
GAME?

THE WARRIORS GAME IS
DVR'ed, AS I WAS HOPING
TO ENJOY IT LATER, UNSPOILED
BY KNOWLEDGE OF ITS OUTCOME.
MAY I ASK WHY YOUR ARMS
ARE RAISED?

YOGA MOVE.

THIS YOGA MOVE
IS CALLED
'DOWNWARD
BAT.'

HEY,
GOTTA
GO DO
MORE
YOGA.

I'm a big-time fan of the Golden State Warriors and have a friend who does this to me all the time. After a whole day of going out of my way to not look at the scores, I'll hear the DING of an incoming text, reflexively check my phone, and see a text that says, "HOW DID THE WARRIORS BLOW THIS??"

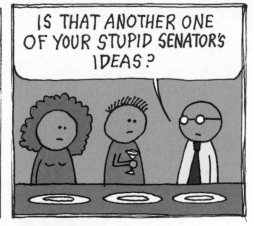

I had the guy say "stupid senator" in the fifth panel instead of "stupid president," because if I had said the latter, it could only have been then-President Biden. And then my email box would be filled with long, angry emails. And while I'm not afraid of complaints, it wasn't the point of the strip.

Anyone who would give Pig responsibility for a seven-million-dollar account deserves whatever happens to them.

As I mentioned earlier, I often write the strip as I walk, recording the ideas on the Voice Memos app on my phone. On the recording for this particular strip, as soon as I say, "I punch them with both fists simultaneously," I start laughing really hard. I enjoy my job far too much.

I think this particular pose of a happy, wide-mouthed Pig marching off is my favorite one to draw.

I'm the only cartoonist I know who draws on a flat desk, as opposed to all the other cartoonists who draw on tilted drafting tables. I've drawn on it for so many years that the wood is wearing down (see photo on next page). And yes, I still use a manual pencil sharpener.

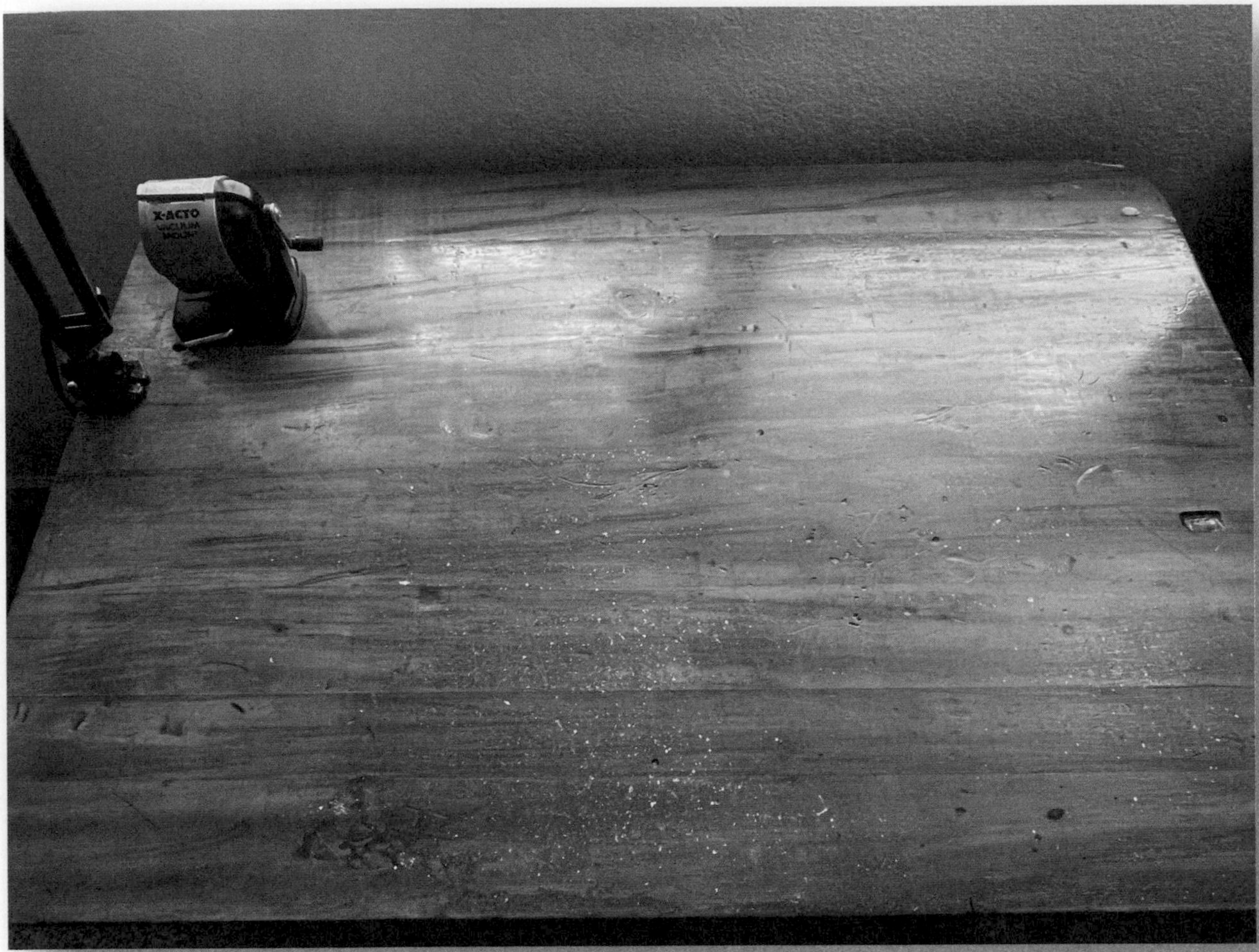
X-ACTO

When this strip ran, I got a number of emails and messages that looked like these two:

"Today's (12/25/22) comic was one of the first play on words from you that I didn't understand."

"I delight in all your punning punishments and have never felt blown
to the wayside of comprehension until this morning."

So for all the poor people I confused, Pig's line in the second-to-last panel is based on the
Beach Boys's song lyric, "I wish they all could be California girls."

216

I still occasionally hear of offended readers writing to their newspapers because they do not like the word "ass" appearing on the comics page. But it is another word for donkey.

Whenever I get really tense (usually before a big book tour), my back goes out. Sometimes it's so bad I can barely stand.

217

My hobby is travel, usually to somewhere a bit challenging or unusual. This is a photo I took at the Angkor Wat temple complex during a recent trip to Cambodia:

Whenever I do a strip like this, I will almost always get at least one complaint from someone offended by what they view as my making light of guns. I do it anyway.

The one thing that I'll always remember from the early part of the COVID era was going to the grocery store in dishwashing gloves, afraid to touch anything. Then I'd carefully peel them off before driving home, where I'd wash both the gloves and my hands for at least two minutes. It was only later that we all found out that the virus was airborne and started wearing masks. Looking back at that time, it all feels like madness.

I sometimes do block people who go out of their way to say annoying things on my social media feeds. It makes me feel all-powerful, like a whimsical king shouting, "Off with their heads!"

Another bald human in *Pearls*. It's like a daily ad for Rogaine.

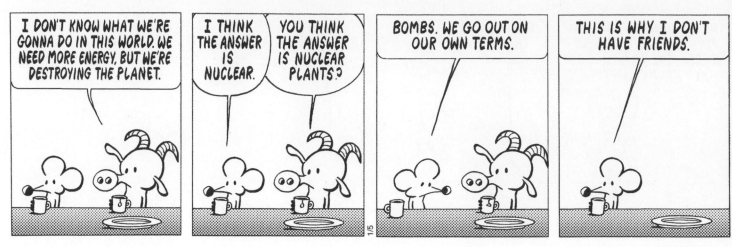

During a recent trip to Pennsylvania, I made a point of visiting Three Mile Island, the site of a terrifying nuclear accident in 1979. Below is a photo I took:

From the Department of Strange but True: Not only did I not wear a seatbelt, but one time when I was a little kid, the passenger door wasn't fully closed, and when my mother started driving away, I fell out of the car and rolled to the curb. Maybe she *did* want to kill me.

I think I've only ever drawn Wise Ass sitting up on his hill. Maybe in future strips I should explore his personal life and have it be reckless and filled with stupid decision-making.

One month after this strip appeared, *Dilbert* cartoonist Scott Adams was dropped from newspapers for comments he made about race.

It's fun sometimes to break the fourth wall like this and have the characters realize they're just drawings.

I really have nothing against cyclists, but I do get a little tired of them telling me to stop making fun of them. So I made sure to include them in "annoying guy bingo."

Sometimes I hurt cyclists' feelings. Like when I include them in "annoying guy bingo."

I notice the negative bent of the news most often when I travel. You hear all these terrible things about a country and then you go there and it's wonderful.

I ran this on my actual birthday, January 16. Now that you know that, there is no excuse for not sending presents.

In the early days of *Pearls*, the strip got sold into some newspapers in non-English-speaking countries. But it didn't work, because translations of strips like this didn't make sense. Heck, it often doesn't make sense to people who *do* speak English.

I hate having to put these fake phone numbers in strips, but if I put a real one, some unknown person is going to get inundated with calls. Which I have to admit would amuse me.

I thought Rat's line in the second panel was kind of clever. Also, you can't stop me from complimenting myself.

I did this strip after being on the treadmill at the gym and noticing I had burned only ten calories. Granted, I just stood there with the power off, but still, it was disappointing.

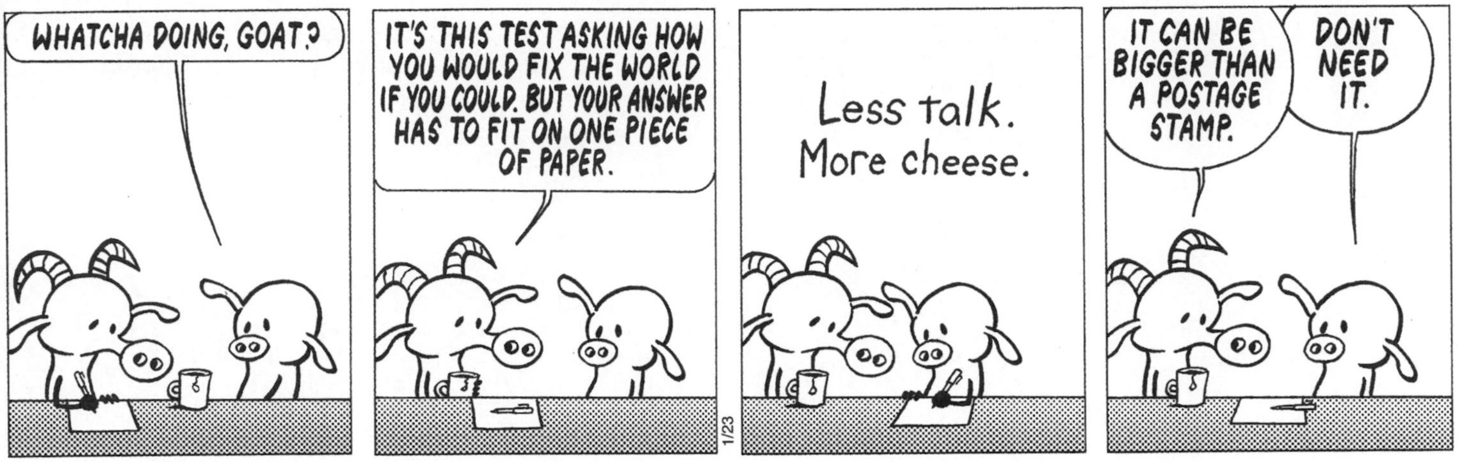
WHATCHA DOING, GOAT?
IT'S THIS TEST ASKING HOW YOU WOULD FIX THE WORLD IF YOU COULD. BUT YOUR ANSWER HAS TO FIT ON ONE PIECE OF PAPER.
Less talk. More cheese.
1/23
IT CAN BE BIGGER THAN A POSTAGE STAMP.
DON'T NEED IT.

I used to buy big packages of 20 or so individually wrapped string cheeses for my studio. But I would eat every single one the first day. Which may explain why I have trouble burning off calories.

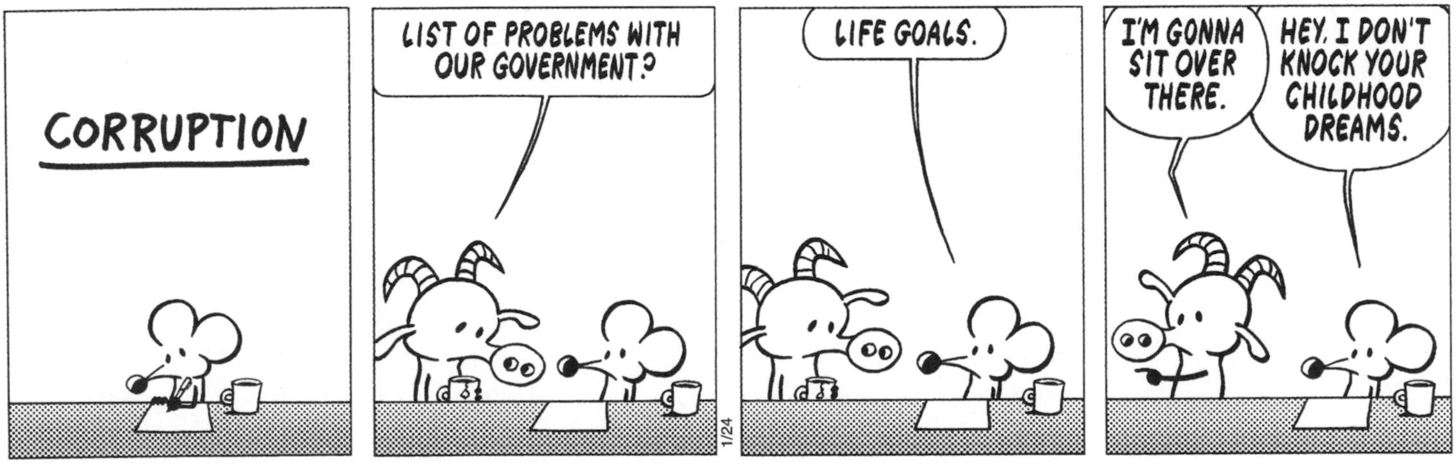
CORRUPTION
LIST OF PROBLEMS WITH OUR GOVERNMENT?
1/24
LIFE GOALS.
I'M GONNA SIT OVER THERE.
HEY, I DON'T KNOCK YOUR CHILDHOOD DREAMS.

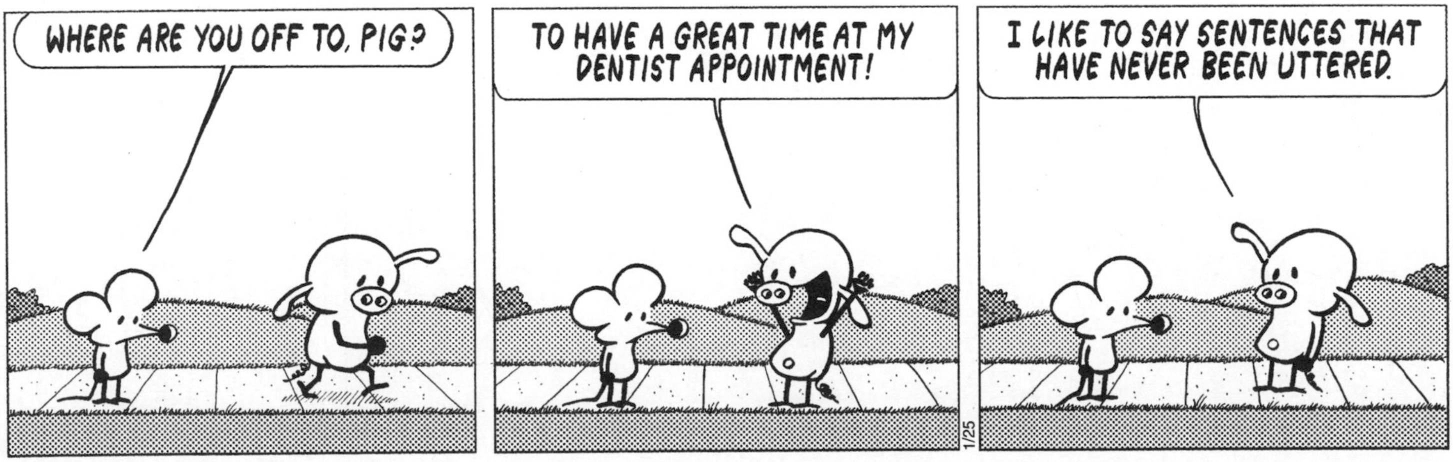
WHERE ARE YOU OFF TO, PIG?
TO HAVE A GREAT TIME AT MY DENTIST APPOINTMENT!
1/25
I LIKE TO SAY SENTENCES THAT HAVE NEVER BEEN UTTERED.

I was recently told by my dentist that I had to get a tooth removed. So a few weeks later I went to the oral surgeon, who, just before starting the procedure, noticed that the dentist's office had identified the wrong tooth for removal. I left and have not been back.

If you're keeping track at home, this is the third strip this week where a character is writing something. I am nothing if not consistent.

I generally don't get offended when someone insults me. Especially if it's clever. My first reaction is usually, "I wish I'd thought of that."

When *Pearls* first started, there were a few more established cartoonists who questioned whether or not it should be in newspapers. They criticized the drawing style, the dark nature of the strip, and United Media's decision to syndicate it. Twenty-three years later, the strip is in over 800 newspapers.

Group texts should be illegal. They are the bane of my existence.

Hot Cartooning Tip No. 242: For whatever reason, short words that begin with a "B" are generally funnier words (e.g., belch, burp, boob, butt, bob, bum, bump, blimp).

In some strips, the top of Rat's head comes up to about my knee, while in other strips (like this one), he is more than half my height, meaning that my size in the strip varies considerably. This is an intentional artistic choice designed to reflect my relative self-esteem on any given day.

Note regarding my prior comment: Fine, I just screwed up. But for a moment, you thought that I was pretty profound.

This strip was in response to a story that NBA star Kyrie Irving was questioning whether the world was round or flat. The level of stupidity required for that is rather mind-blowing.

Absoflutist: A person who believes that one flutist should hold all the power.

As I mentioned before, I color the Sunday *Pearls* but do not color the daily strips, and I typically don't even see them before they're published. As a result, errors sometimes happen, which was the case with the colorized version of this strip. The joke was supposed to be that Rat built a wall right down the middle of the house, which would be very odd. But the colorist put the characters outside in the second and third panels (below), and an outdoor wall is not odd at all.

I recently took an unsteady kayak ride in a New Orleans bayou, only to find out later that the bayou (which is right in the middle of the city) can often be filled with alligators. I'm including the story of that incident in a travel book I'm currently working on.

Years ago, I used to end these strips with Goat grimacing in frustration, which I now think shows a certain lack of confidence on my part (i.e., Rat just did something funny. And if you don't believe me, just look at Goat's reaction). So I now try to avoid that whenever possible, because the joke should be able to stand on its own.

In fairness, the word "literally" has become so misused that Webster's now includes the following definition: "Used in an exaggerated way to emphasize a statement or description that is not literally true or possible."

I really do have a cousin Nick. Once when we were little kids, he kicked me in the testicles and locked himself in the bathroom for the rest of the day. I got him back weeks later by inviting him over to my house, where I hid atop the roof and used a slingshot to pelt him with acorns. Ah, family.

My wife Staci goes through our credit card bill every month, and one time after I took a trip, she noticed two $62.50 charges from a bar that were back-to-back on the bill. So she asked me to call the bar and tell them they accidentally charged me twice, at which point I had to tell her that no, I had purposely ordered the exact same round of drinks twice in quick succession. Ah, drinking.

Note regarding my last comment to any children that may be reading this: Drinking is more fun if you hide it from your spouse.

One of my favorite stats from nature: Squirrels fail to find almost 3/4 of the acorns they bury.

I don't have anything specific to say about this strip, so I'll just say here that my favorite color is blue.

There's a great bestselling book that was recently published about how to talk to people that may not agree with you politically. It's called *I Never Thought of It That Way* by Mónica Guzmán. More importantly, her son Julian is a fan of *Pearls*.

When I used to get really depressed (doesn't happen quite as much anymore), I would sometimes sit in a dark closet. Something about the solitude and darkness made me feel better.

I liked the notion of the panel being like a soft screen that could be pulled down like this.

I've been to Finland. It wasn't that happy.

There is a real debate about what "SPAM" actually stands for. One person wrote me to say it is an acronym for "some parts are meat." The Hormel Foods Corporation has said it stood for "Shoulder of Pork and Ham." Members of the SPAM Museum in Austin, Minnesota, have said it stands for "Specially Produced American Meat." And yes, the takeaway here is that SPAM has

Panel 1: WHAT'S THE MATTER WITH YOU?

Panel 2: NEIGHBOR BOB WAS JUST IN HERE AND HE SAID HE WAS OFF TO TALK TO A HAMBURGER AND A FRANKFURTER.

Panel 3: YEAH, THEY'RE HIS FRIENDS FROM GERMANY. ONE'S FROM HAMBURG AND ONE'S FROM FRANKFURT.

Panel 4: KNOWLEDGE RUINS ALL OF LIFE'S FUN.

Hamburg is a seaport in northern Germany where in the 1960s, the Beatles spent the better part of two years really learning how to play as a band. I recently went there to see the Indra Club, one of the last remaining places where the Beatles played. I'm the shady character loitering in front of the entrance.

The only reason I have the characters speak from behind a wall is because Charlie Brown and Linus used to do it in *Peanuts*. If you think about it, it's sort of an odd place for two people to have a conversation.

247

Believe it or not, the neighbor who lives on the other side of our fence is named Bob. I never thought he read the strip, but apparently he does, as he came up to me at a neighborhood party and said he knew the strip had a Neighbor Bob in it. The truth is that the character in the strip is not based on him.

Note regarding that last comment: My lawyer made me say that.

Hey, the singular form of dice *is* "die." Which doesn't exactly sound promising.

Have you ever met one of those people who have the old-fashioned telephone ring as their ringtone? It's very annoying and makes me question their judgment in life.

This really is the way our system works. Except they don't call them bribes. They call them "campaign donations."

This was an actual rumor making the rounds during the time of the COVID vaccine. Sometimes the absurdity of real life gets ahead of my ability to make fun of it.

Every year since my son Thomas was very young, we would go to Lake Tahoe, Nevada for a father/son trip. The first time we did it, I bet on a baseball game in one of the casinos and we won big. So we did it every year thereafter, and lost every single time. It's important to get your children hooked on gambling early.

Goat sure has a lot of time to stand around doing nothing. Perhaps I should give him a job.

Speaking of good books, I recently sat down with a book that I absolutely loved called *Killers of the Flower Moon* by David Grann. It's a murder mystery, but it's based on a true event.

Of all my characters, I think Larry is the most fun to draw. He's really just a series of half-circles (the round bumps on his head, the back of his head, the area around his nostrils, his lips, his belly). I think something about curved linework makes a character more appealing.

This was a popular strip.

While I occasionally have these school dreams, the one I have the most often is that I'm visiting my old law firm and get approached by one of the partners. He tells me that I haven't turned in my billable hours for the last 23 years and that he'd like them by the end of the day. So I frantically try to fill in my timesheets, only to then wake up, sweating and scared.

254

There really is a lot of good out there. But none of it involves my former law firm, to whom I owe 23 years of billable hours.

I often listen to Adele's "Someone Like You" when I write. And I don't care who knows it.

The wide range of emails I have in my inbox from both cyclists and non-cyclists is incredible. A random sampling:

"Why do you portray Jef the cyclist as a smug, condescending, jerk? Did you have an unpleasant experience with cyclists at some point in your life? Most of the mountain bikers and road bikers that I know are decent, normal, people."

"Jeff the cyclist is so spot on. I've been a FedEx courier for 31 years (and) those as$&@"s are the bane of my existence."

"I have enjoyed riding my bike for over 40 years. I guess you could call me a 'cyclist'. Despite that, 'arrogant' is a word that very few would use to describe me. Every time I go for a ride I pray that some motorist does not decide to 'teach me a lesson' for having the gall to ride my bike on his road. I believe your comic strip from last Sunday could make such behavior more acceptable."

"Brilliant shot at cyclists. May they all get hemorrhoids."

Pig's bed needs a headboard. Otherwise, it looks like his pillow is just floating in space. Also, I pronounce pillow "PELL-ow."

This strip was based on a conversation I had with a journalist at a newspaper who said his career was now mostly dependent on how many clicks his stories got.

I have found that more and more I like traveling alone. I get to go wherever I want, whenever I want. And if I want to talk to someone, I just start up a conversation at a bar or café. Usually, the other person asks me to shut the $#@% up, but still, it's a conversation.

I have known people who do this. One of them is my niece, Elenique. It drives me nutters, which I think only encourages her.

I recently traveled for two weeks all through Texas, which I loved, but there was a part of me that was always concerned about guns and mass shootings. Sure enough, on the last day of the trip, there was a mass shooting in the town that I was in that killed nine people.

How goes it, Neighbor Jim?

Good. I've concluded that the key to life is setting big goals and achieving them. Personally. Professionally. Academically. How about you?

I've concluded that all I need is my dog.

Those poor achievers.

Sometimes when my dog Total and I are lying in a grass field together, I use her rear end as a pillow. She finds it very insulting.

Hullo, zeeba neighba... Leesten... Crocs offer nice room for rent on Airbeebee... You is want?

Sure, lemme just check your reviews online first... Oh, look, you have a zero rating and one review...'Host ate my cousin.'

Internet is terrible place.

Hullo zeeba neighba. Crocs want know if you want rent room we has on Airbeebee.

You have a review from an antelope saying you ate his cousin. Good hosts at least respond to reviews like that.

We is respond. Check site.

'Yum' is not a response.

Gee. Whuh you want from us?

I generally prefer Airbnb to hotels, mostly because I get more space and can wash my clothes. But every now and then it goes awry, like on a recent trip to Puerto Rico, where at 7 a.m., someone started drilling on the other side of my bedroom wall.

THUD
THUD
THUD
THUD

RAT, IT'S ALMOST MIDNIGHT. WHAT ARE YOU DOING?

RUNNING IN PLACE. I HAVE TO GET IN MY 10,000 STEPS FOR THE DAY.

WHAT HAPPENS IF YOU DON'T?

ALL OF LIFE FALLS APART AND SOCIETY DEVOLVES INTO CHAOS.

NOW I FEEL BAD FOR INTERRUPTING.

I really did this while in a hotel room in Philadelphia. It was 11:50 p.m. and I noticed I had done 9.9 miles of walking for the day. So I got up and ran back and forth across the room until I hit 10 miles.

WHAT ARE YOU DOING, PIG?

LOOKING AT THIS FOOD PYRAMID I HAD TO MAKE. IT'S SUPPOSED TO HELP YOU MAINTAIN A HEALTHY, BALANCED DIET.

CAN I SEE IT?

SURE.

GOUDA
BRIE | FETA
PARMESAN | CHEDDAR
MOZZARELLA

MIGHT NOT BE ACCURATE.

YEAH, LEFT OFF SWISS.

DO YOU REMEMBER THE COMIC 'THE FAR SIDE'?

OF COURSE I DO. IT WAS MY FAVORITE.

WELL, I HAVE IT ON GOOD AUTHORITY THAT OUR STRIP TODAY IS JUST AS FUNNY AS 'THE FAR SIDE' USED TO BE.

OH, WOW. IT'D BE AN HONOR TO BE IN A STRIP THAT GOOD.

APRIL FOOL'S!

I WISH THEY WOULDN'T DO THAT.

While I have met many of my cartooning influences, from Charles Schulz (*Peanuts*) to Bill Watterson (*Calvin and Hobbes*) to Scott Adams (*Dilbert*) to Berkeley Breathed (*Bloom County*), the one guy I have yet to meet is Gary Larson, the creator of *The Far Side*. I'm still hoping to one day make it happen.

4/2

Most people at my syndicate now work from home at least two days a week. So I never know if I should call their work number or their mobile number. Either way, they always love hearing from me.

 GOOD EVENING AND WELCOME TO THE SIX O'CLOCK NEWS.

 RATHER THAN GIVE YOU THE NEWS TONIGHT, WE THOUGHT WE'D JUST JUMP TO THE PART AT THE END WHERE YOU SAY, 'OH, GOD, HOW MUCH WORSE CAN THINGS GET?'

 GOOD NIGHT, AND HAVE A PLEASANT TOMORROW.

 WHAT A TIME SAVER THAT WAS.

Note from Reed Jackson, Stephan's comic strip editor, regarding that last comment: *I take Stephan's calls only because I'm required to.*

 IN A MOMENT OF GREAT SPIRITUAL DEVELOPMENT, I'VE FINALLY STOPPED JUDGING OTHERS.

 THAT'S GREAT. WHAT WAS THE KEY?

 ACCEPTING THAT EVERYONE ELSE IS A MORON AND THERE'S NOTHING I CAN DO ABOUT IT.

 I THINK THAT'S STILL JUDGING. PLEASE DON'T JUDGE MY PROGRESS.

 HEY, PATTY POSSUM, WE'RE HAVING A BIG BAKE SALE TO RAISE MONEY FOR THE SCHOOL. WE'D LOVE IT IF YOU COULD HELP.

 I HATE WHEN SHE PLAYS DEAD.

I think I might have mentioned this in a prior treasury, but one time when I was speaking at a middle school, a student asked me about my college education. I told him that I went to U.C. Berkeley and became a lawyer, but that if I had known I was going to be a cartoonist, I probably could have dropped out in high school. A teacher then slipped me a note on stage that said, "You've just told an auditorium of young kids to drop out of school. Could you please correct that?" So I did.

I try to go to the gym twice a week, but I dread it every single time.

THE PHASES OF WAITING TO HEAR BACK FROM SOMEONE ON SOMETHING IMPORTANT

BY ME.

RAT

PHASE 1: PATIENCE

It's only been a few days. Give them time.

PHASE 2: EXPLANATIONS

Maybe they're out sick or just busy.

4/9

PHASE 3: DOUBLE-CHECKING

FedEx? I'm calling to see if my package got delivered.

It did.

PHASE 4: SELF-DOUBT

Did I do something wrong?

PHASE 5: SELF-HATRED

I'm a loser and nobody likes me.

PHASE 6: ANGER

THEY'RE LOSERS AND NOBODY LIKES THEM!

PHASE 7: CONSUMED BY VENGEANCE YOU TRY TO PASS OFF AS INDIFFERENCE.

Not that I care or anything, but I hope they fall off a cliff and are eaten by crows.

PHASE EIGHT: USE NATIONAL PLATFORM TO VENT FEELINGS?

WHAT GOOD'S A PLATFORM IF YOU DON'T USE IT?

Hahaha, I'M ALWAYS IN PHASE FIVE.

And lucky for you, you won't hear back from me until the next treasury! I have many family members that envy you.

BONUS SECTION

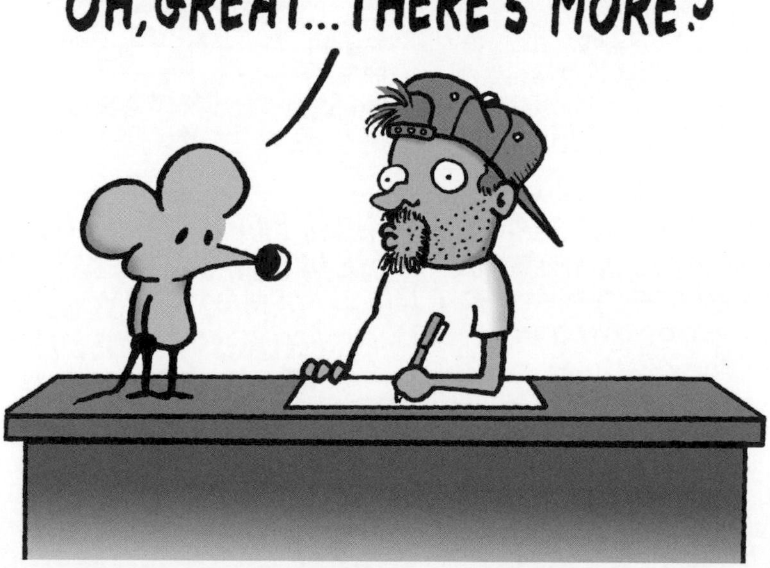
OH, GREAT... THERE'S MORE?

I was having far too much fun going through my old drawings and essays for the introduction to this book but couldn't fit all the ones I wanted into that section.

One of the drawings I found concerned the law school student who had written "STUPID" across one of my first Rat drawings—and it turns out I may not have liked it. For after he wrote what he did, I drew this Rat strip just below it (in which I've blacked-out both the F word and his last name!):

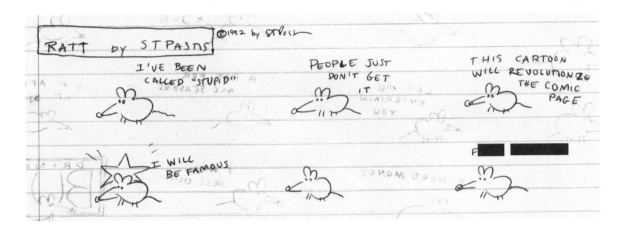

I sort of like that as an obnoxious 24-year-old law student with almost no art skill and what looked like a lifetime of lawyering ahead of me, I was nutters enough to declare, "This cartoon will revolutionize the comic page."

Which may have subconsciously influenced the cover of one of my very first *Pearls* books:

267

But my obnoxiousness was at least consistent throughout the years, as I discovered looking back at this essay I wrote in third grade about my best friend Emilio, questioning his manhood and praising my own:

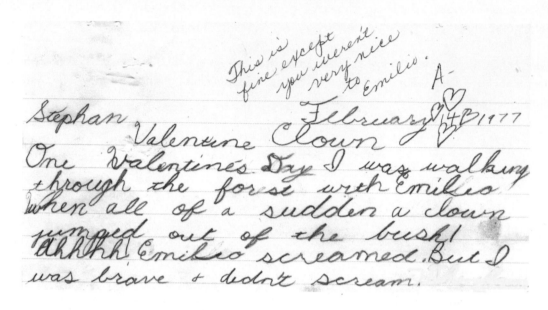

My favorite part is my teacher's comment that, "This is fine except you weren't very nice to Emilio."

The good news is that he recovered, and we are still best friends today:

But perhaps the most intriguing find in my old papers was a phone memo from my grade school office telling me that my mother had called the school. And while the school administrator knew nothing about the subject of the call, she knew *me*, and that was enough for her to write this:

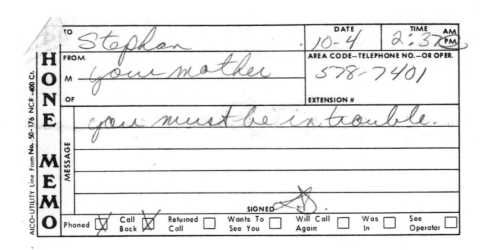

And sadly, she was probably right.

See you in the next treasury.